THE
(NOT SO)
REGULAR MANDALA BOOK

Copyright © 2021-2022 by ArtsyGear

All rights reserved. No part of this publication may be reproduced, distributed, or transmitted in any form or by any means, including photocopying, recording, or other electronic or mechanical methods, without the prior written permission of the publisher, except in the case of brief quotations embodied in critical reviews and certain other noncommercial uses permitted by copyright law. For permission requests, write to the publisher, addressed "Attention: Permissions Coordinator," at the following address: artsygearmerch@gmail.com

This person:

_____

belongs to this Mandala book.

If lost, please contact this book at:

_____

Copyright © 2021-2022 by Artsy Gear. All rights reserved.

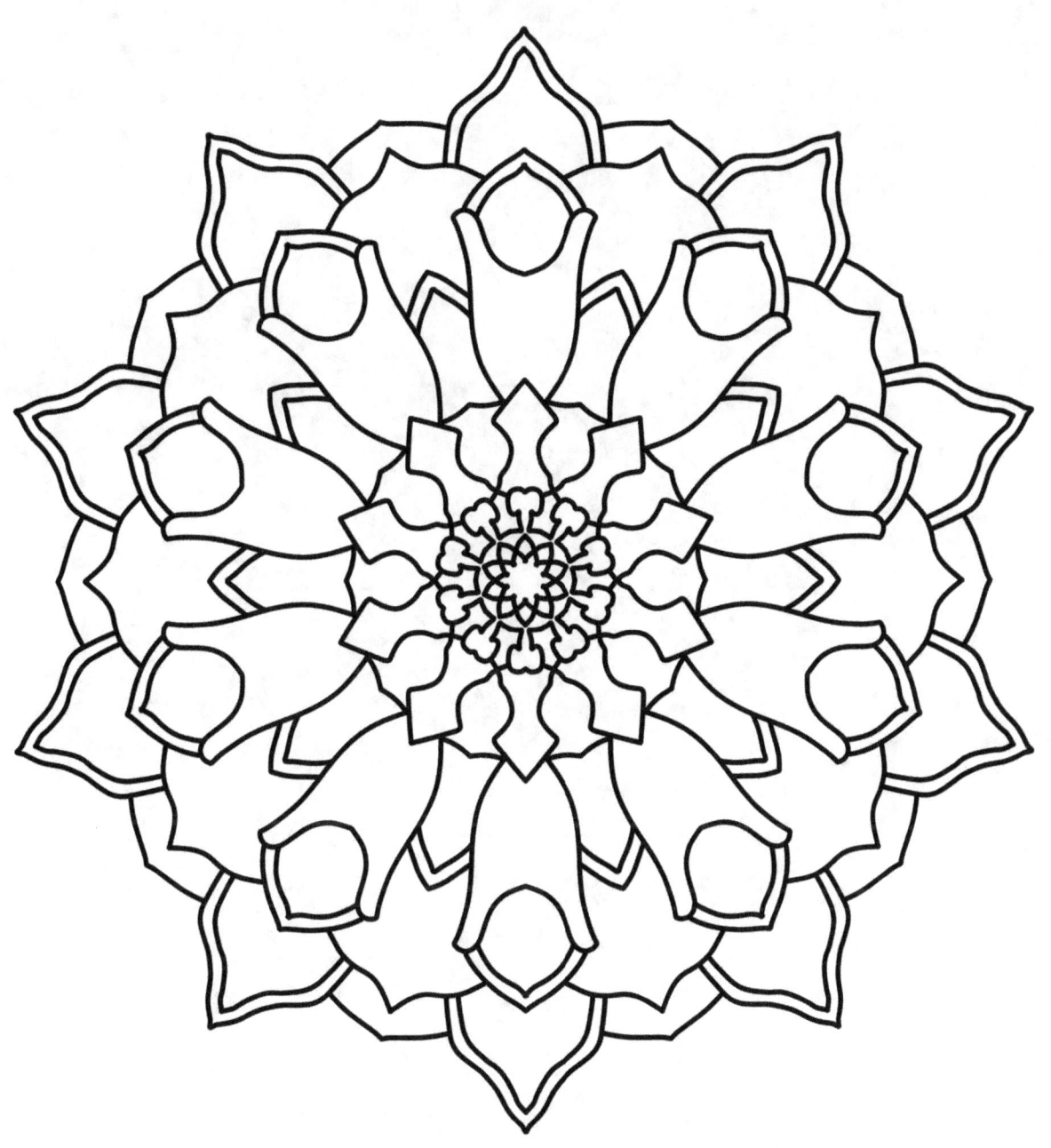

Hi! Nice to meet you. We'll be stuck together for a while, so get comfy and let's get started.

Mandala level: Warm up

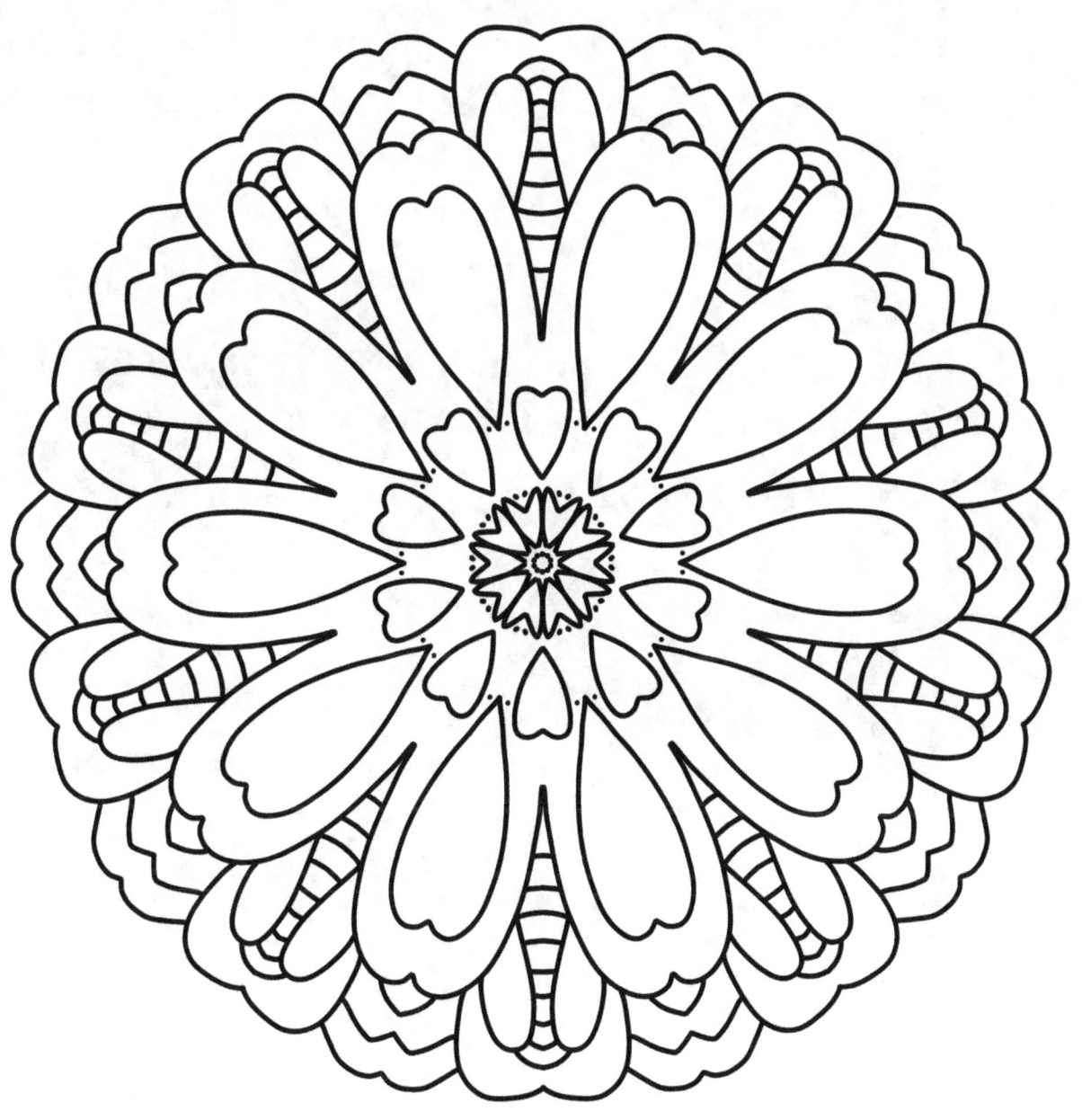

So here's how this is gonna work. You color, I judge. No skipping pages because my dialogue gets all messed up. Also because spoilers, you know? Maybe I have a surprise for you.

Mandala level: Warm up

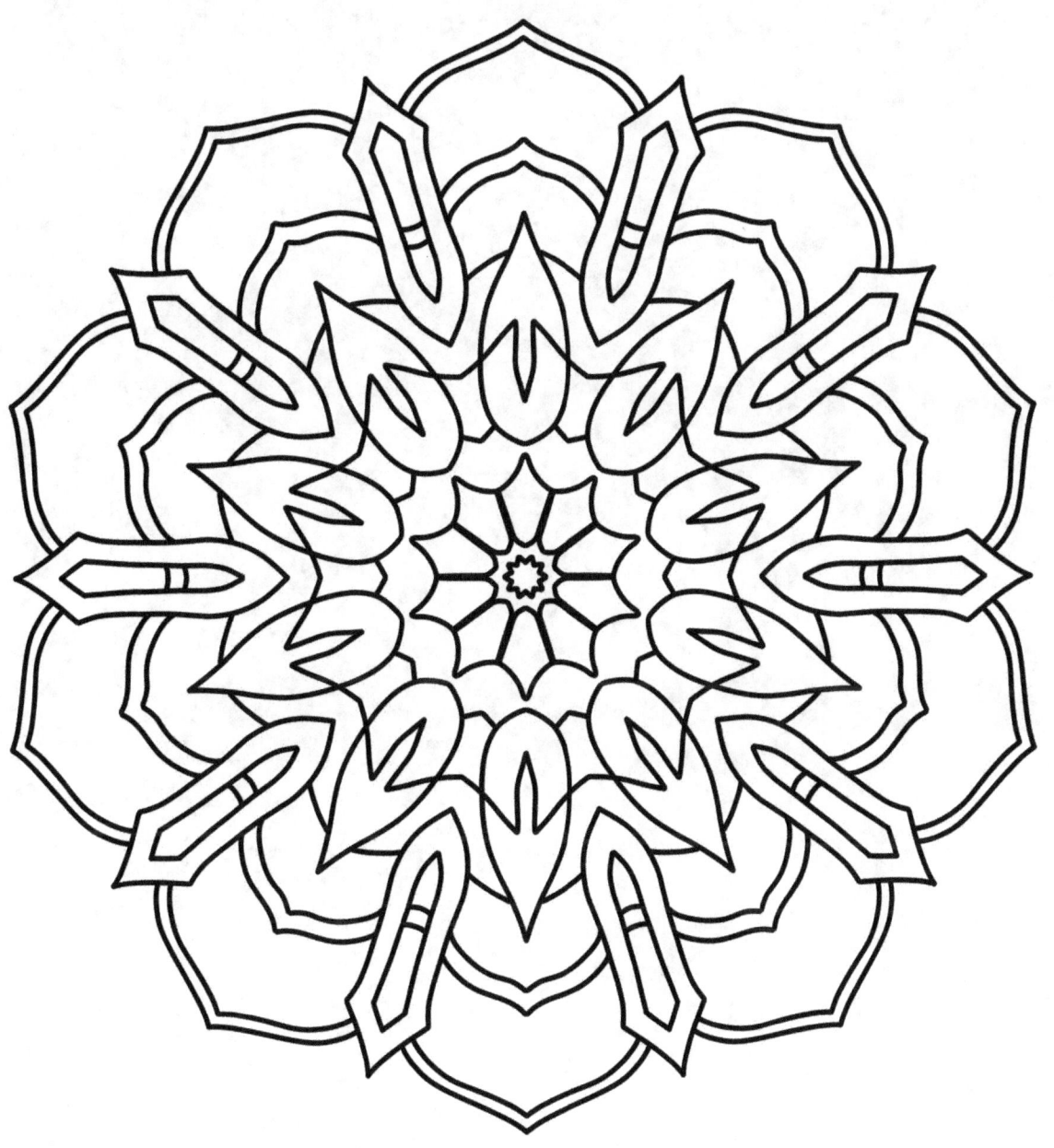

C'mon! Show me what you've got! Time to let all those years in art school shine.

Mandala level: Warm up

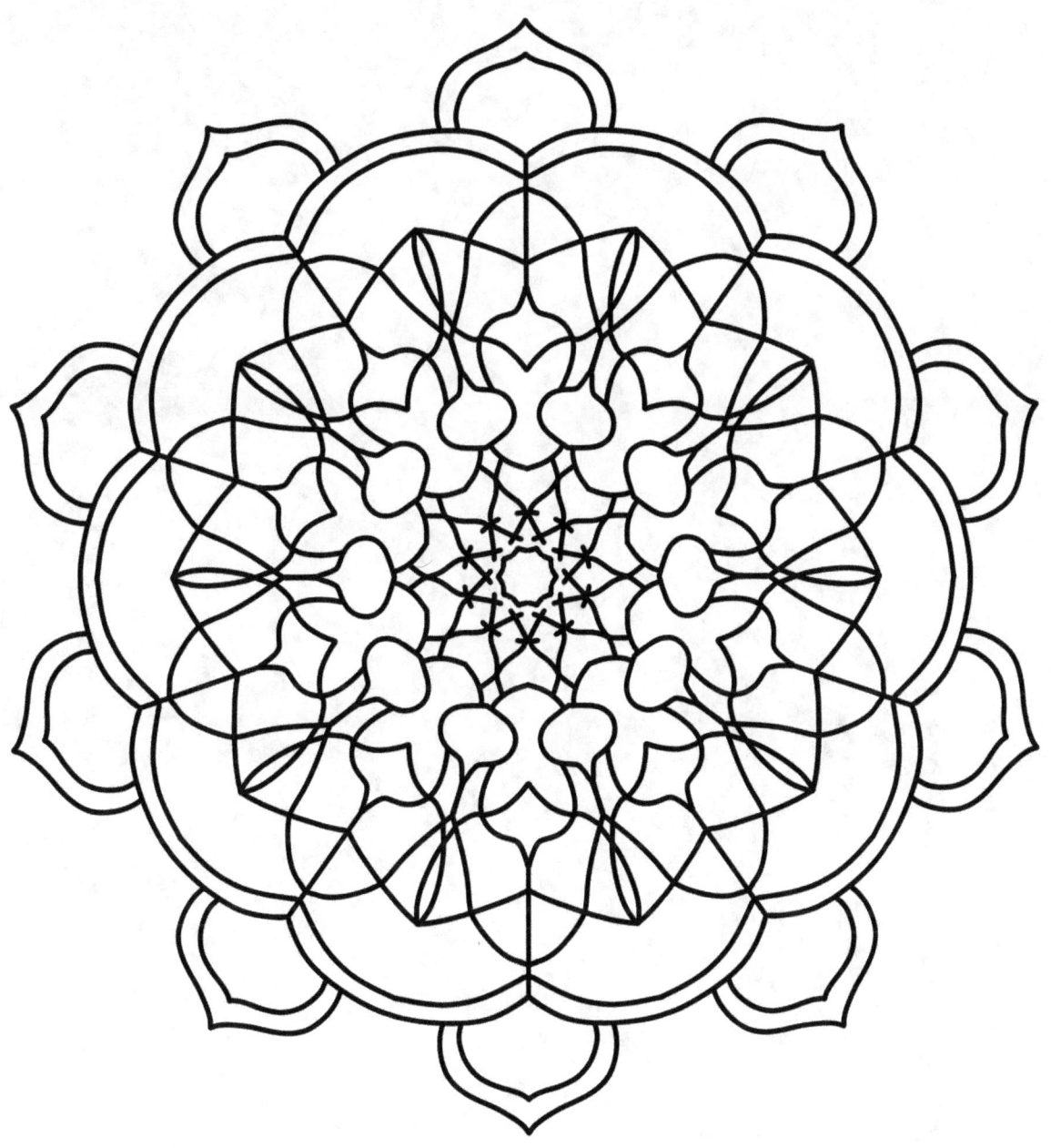

That was okay. I know you can do better on this one.

Mandala level: Warm up

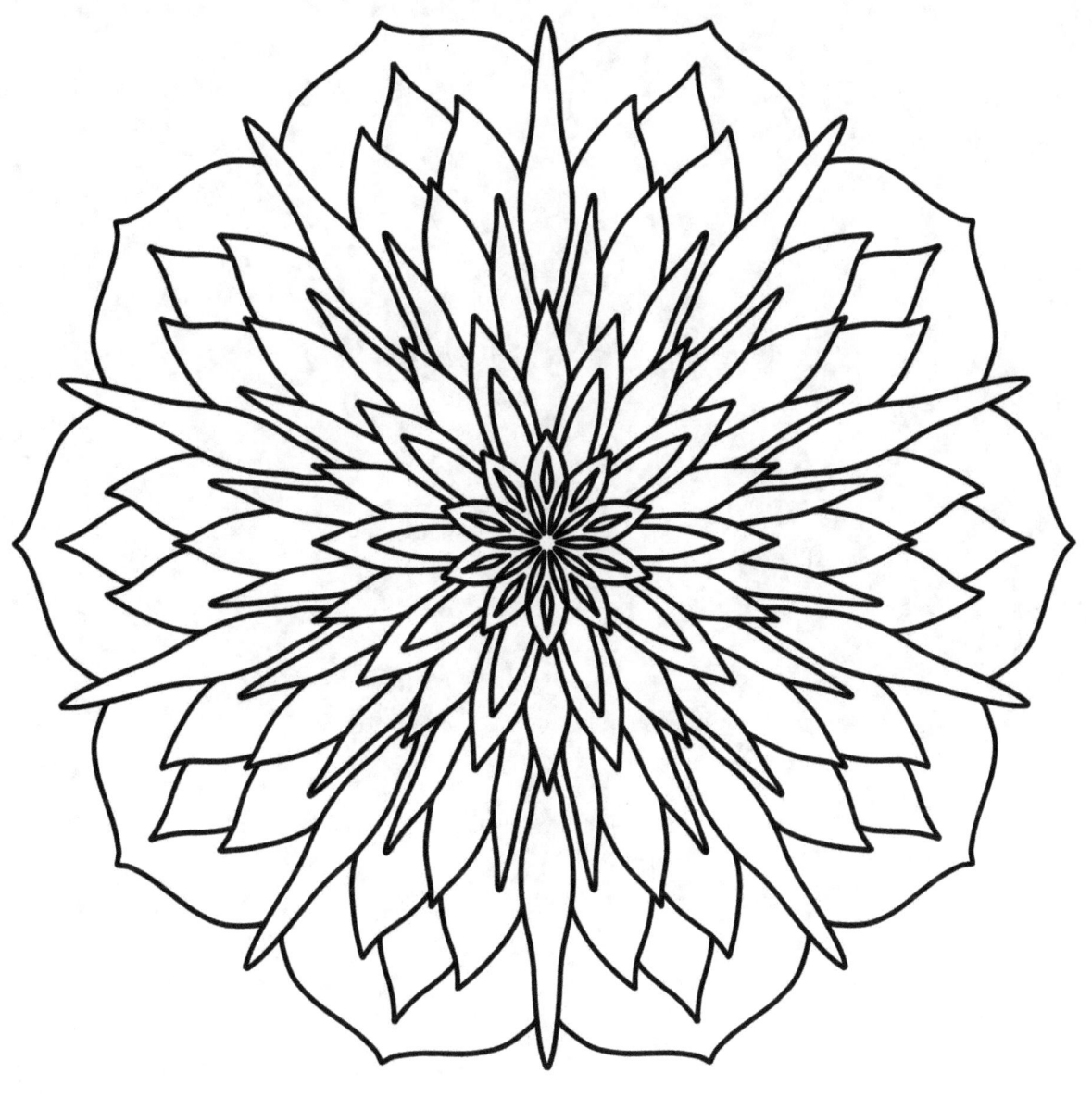

Maybe try to color inside the lines this time?

Mandala level: Warm up

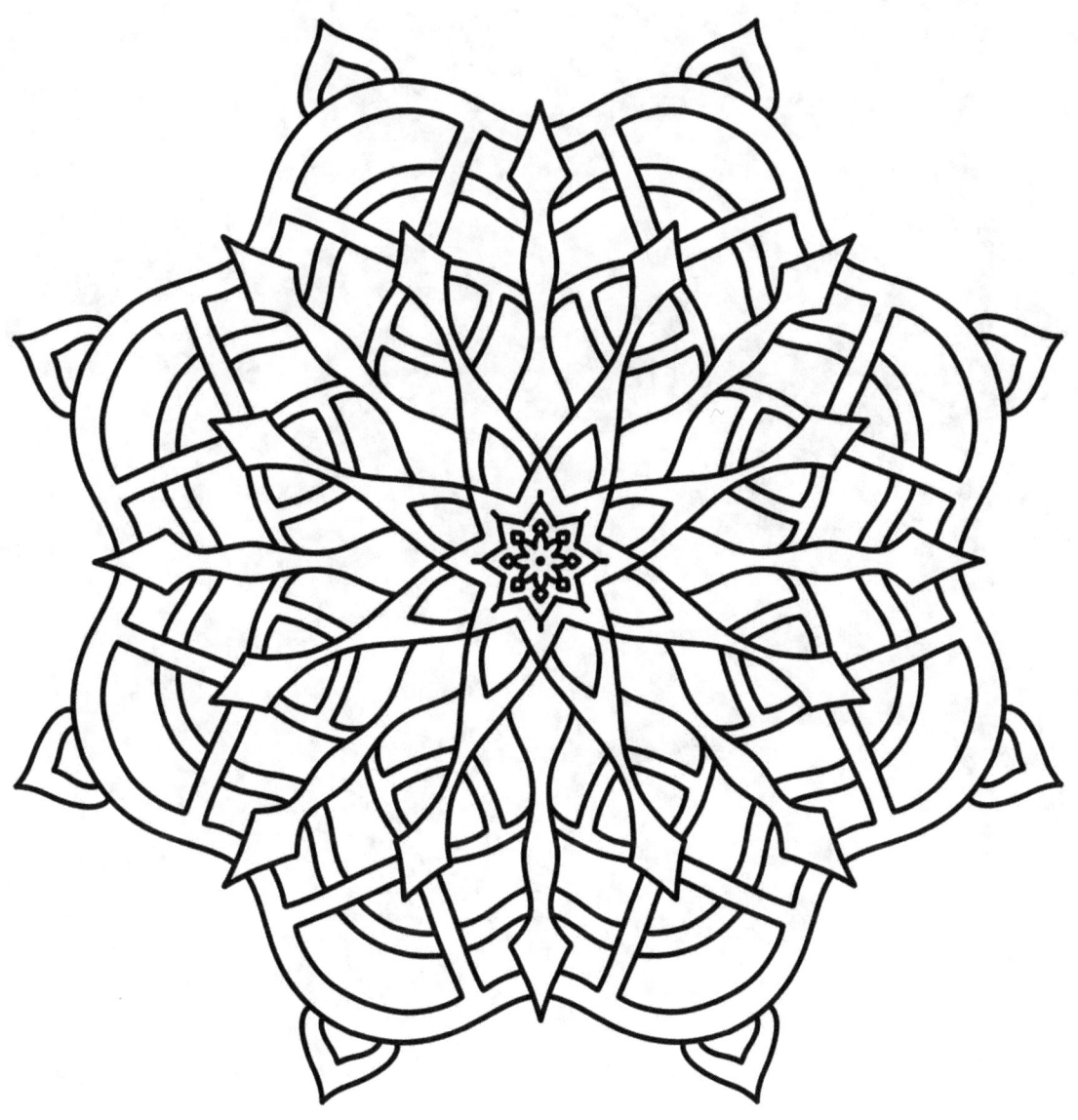

Remember to take breaks between mandalas. I have to catch my breath.

Mandala level: Apprentice

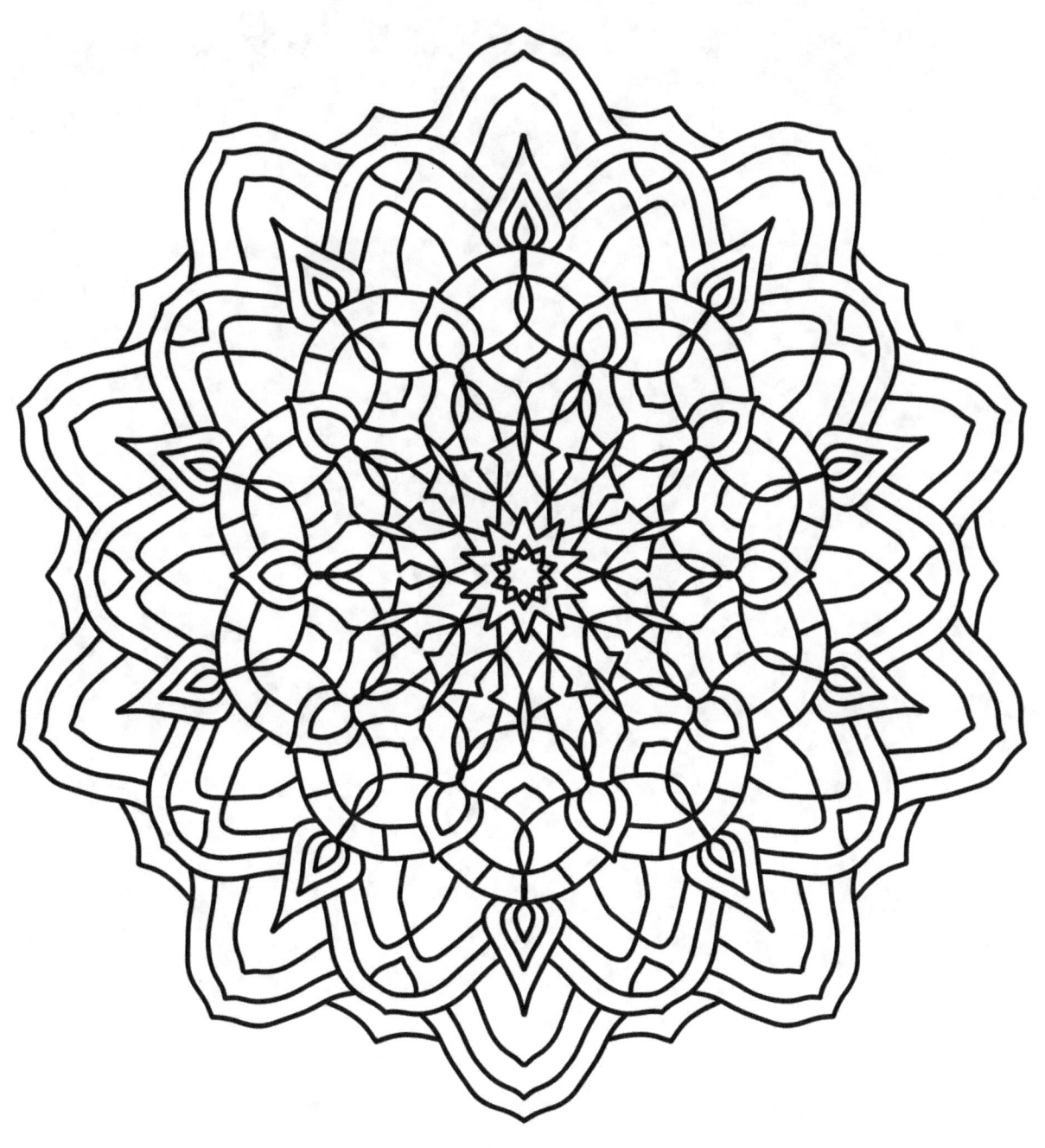

Try not to use red. It gives me headaches.

Mandala level: Apprentice

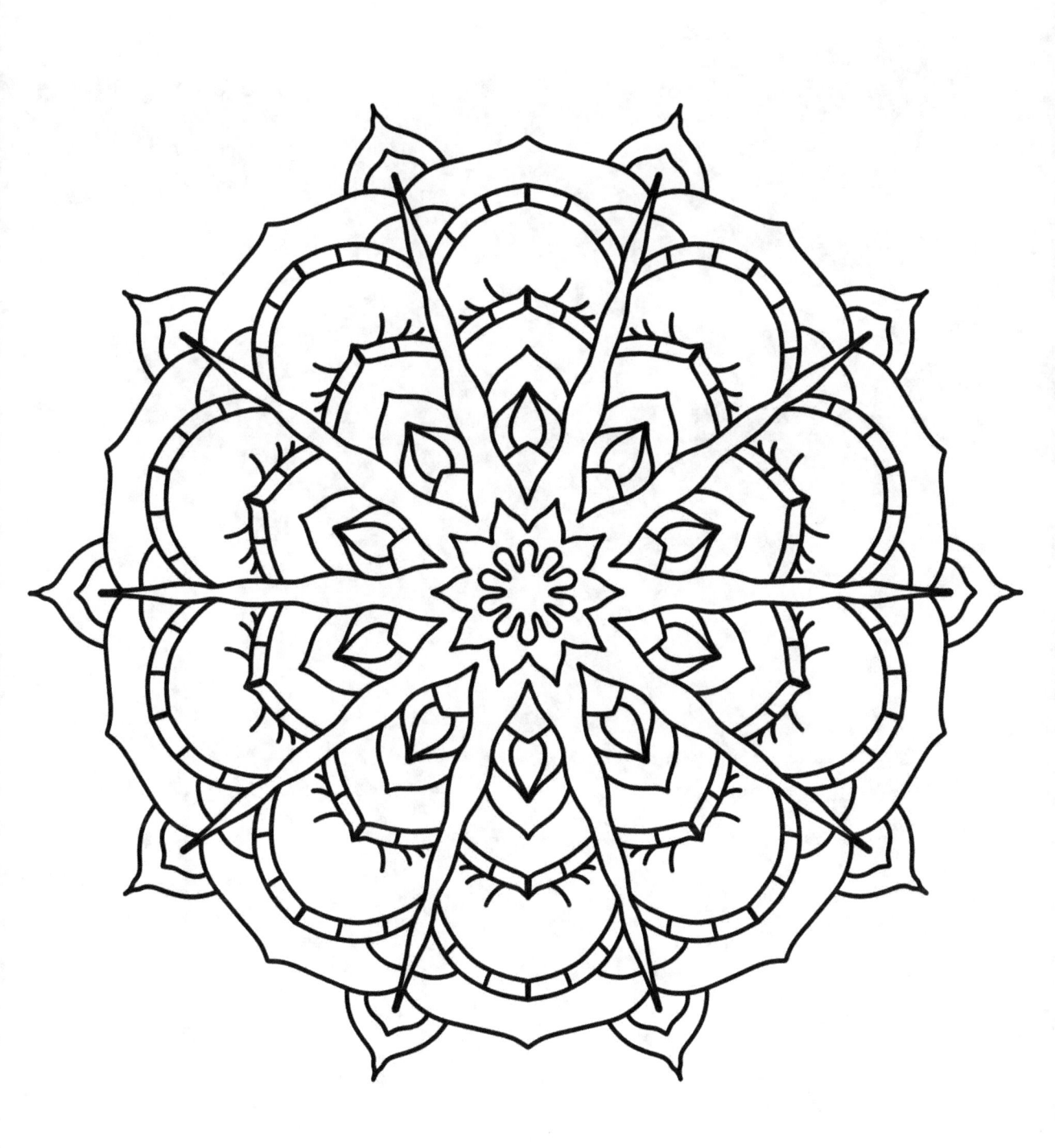

Or use red, whatever; I'm not your dad.

Mandala level: Apprentice

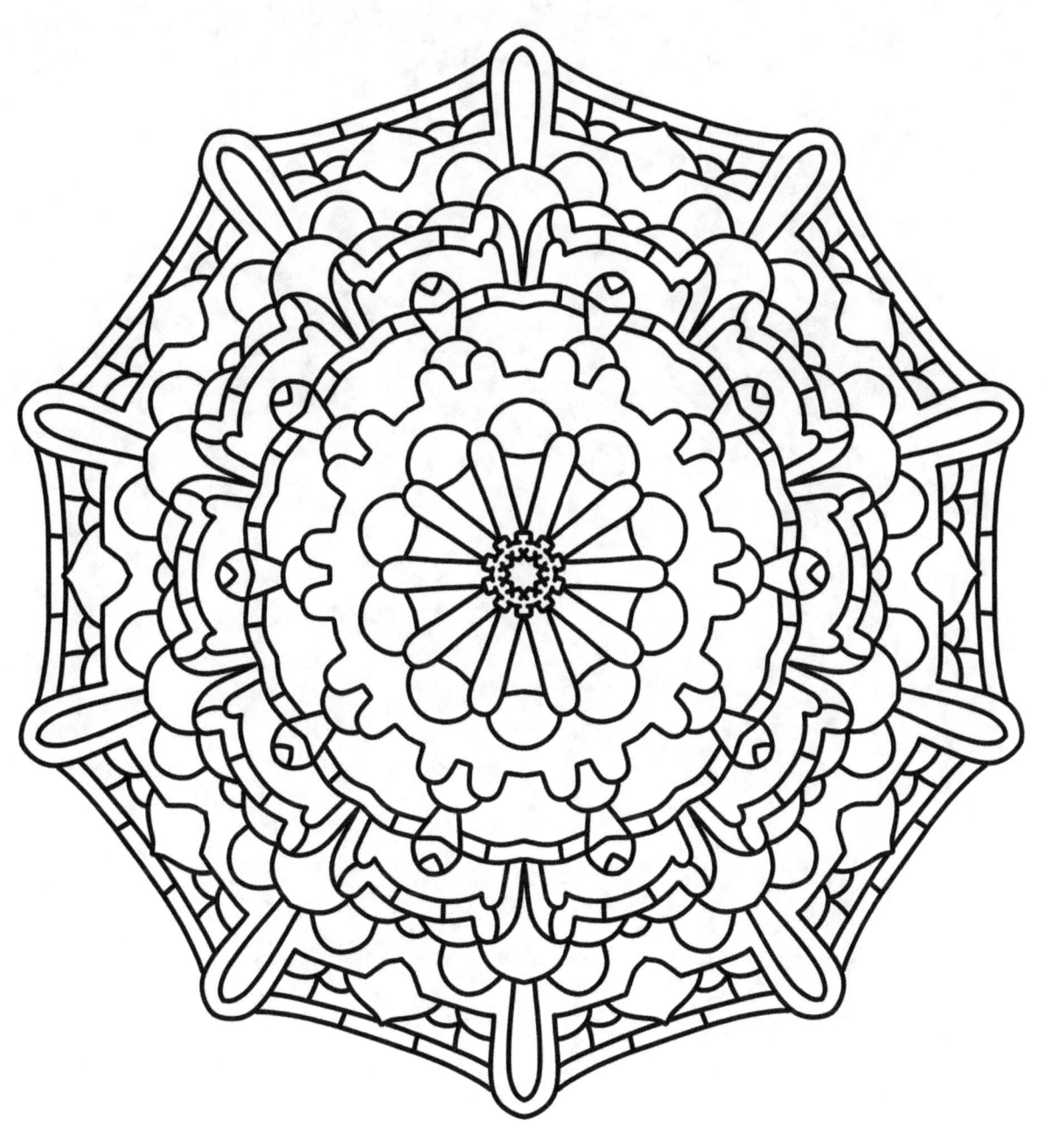

Ok, we're here to relax. I'm sorry.

Mandala level: Apprentice

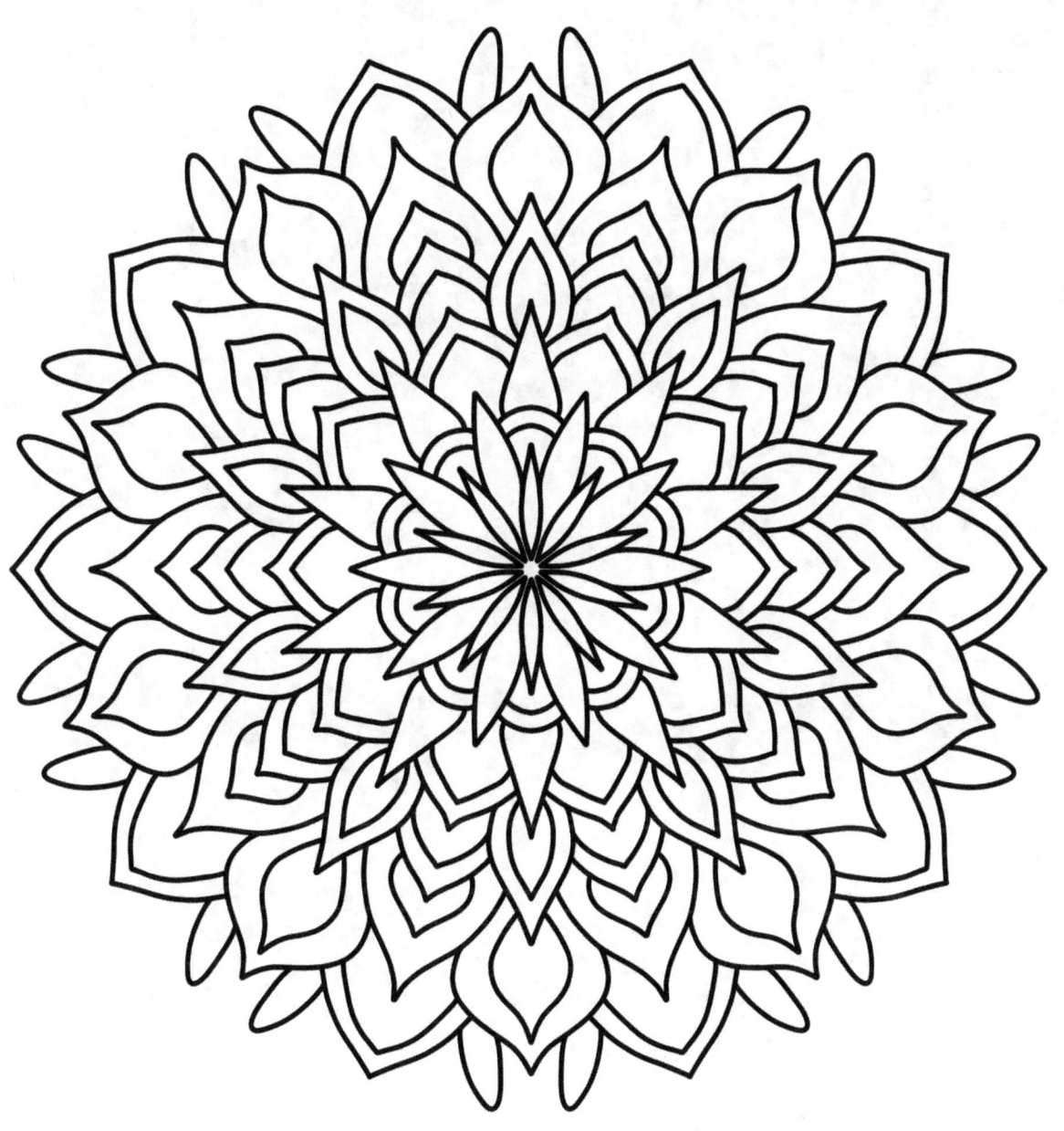

**Have you been drinking enough water today?
I need you hydrated for peak coloring performance.**

Mandala level: Apprentice

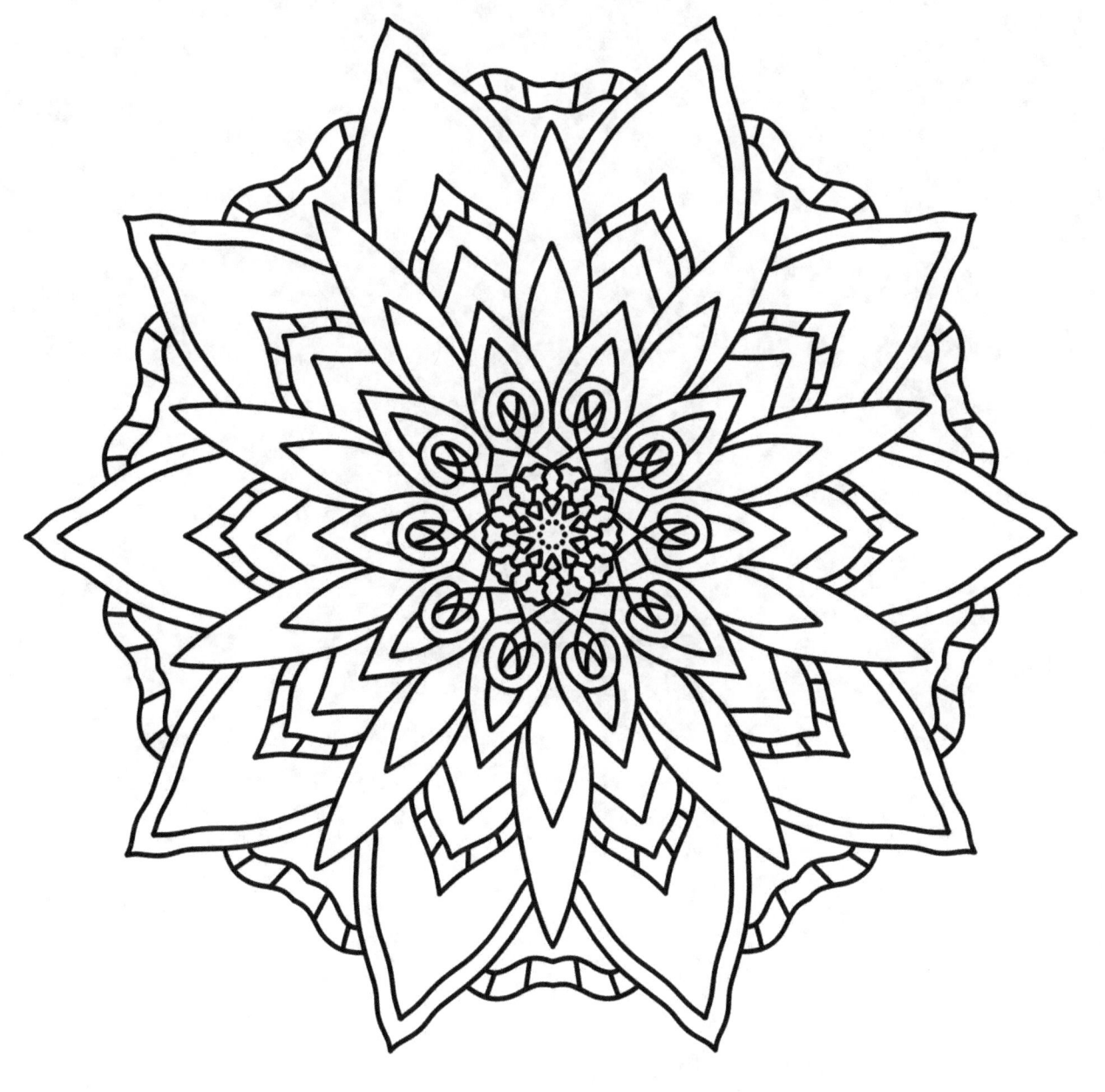

How about I color you, huh?

...

That's what I thought. . .

Mandala level: Apprentice

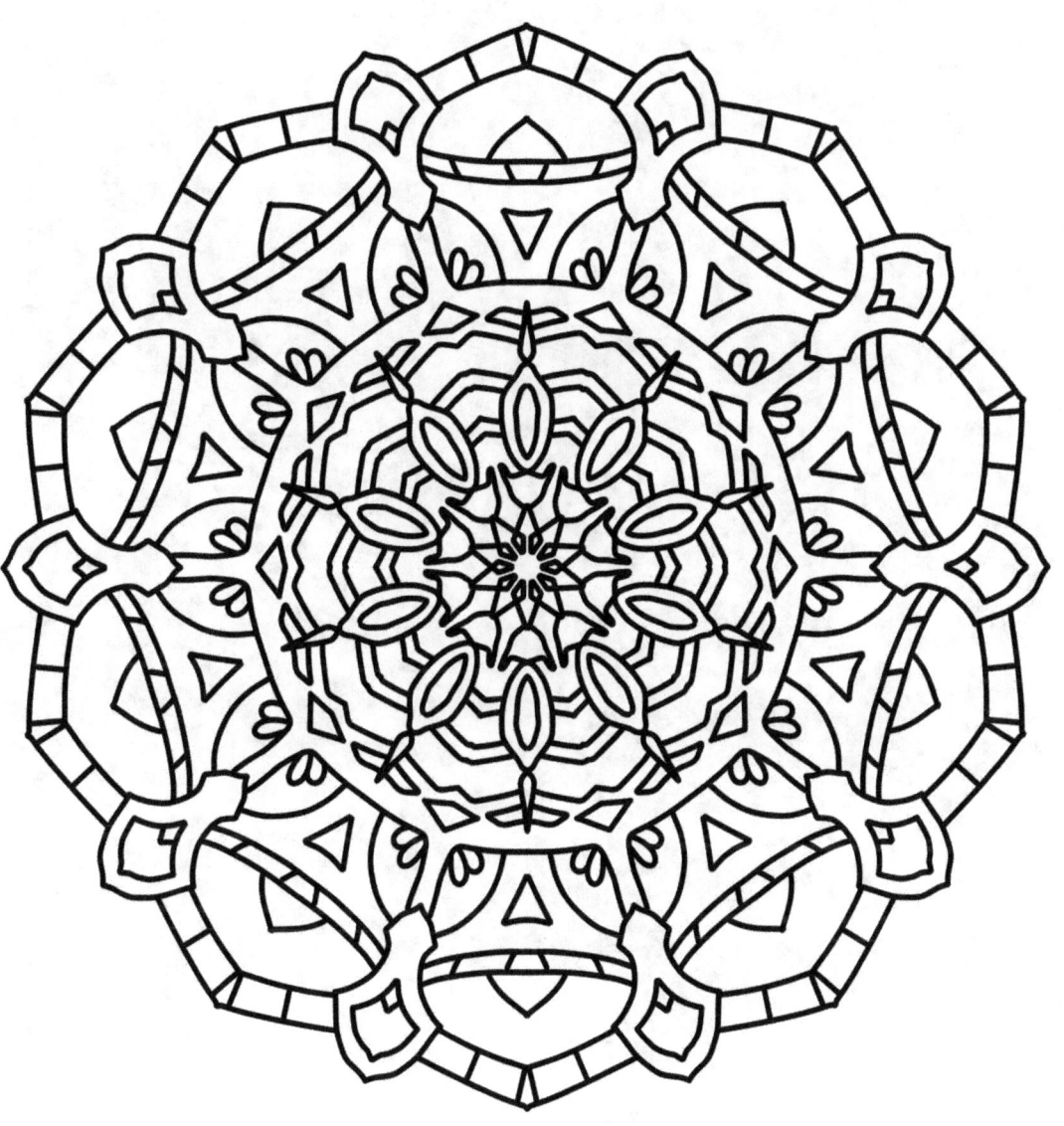

Did you know that if you throw me hard enough I'll come back like a boomerang?

Mandala level: Apprentice

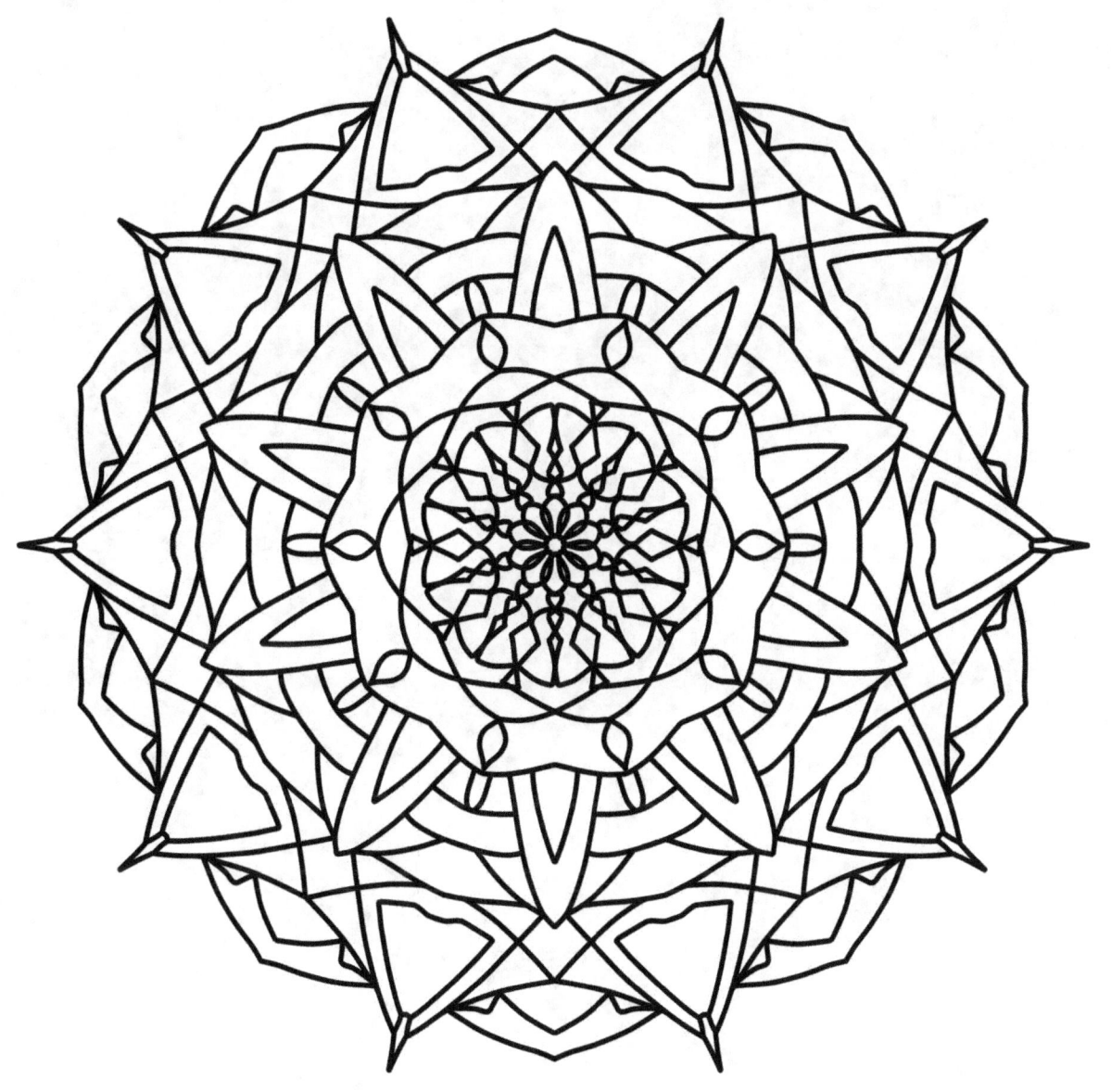

C'mon, give it a try...

Mandala level: Apprentice

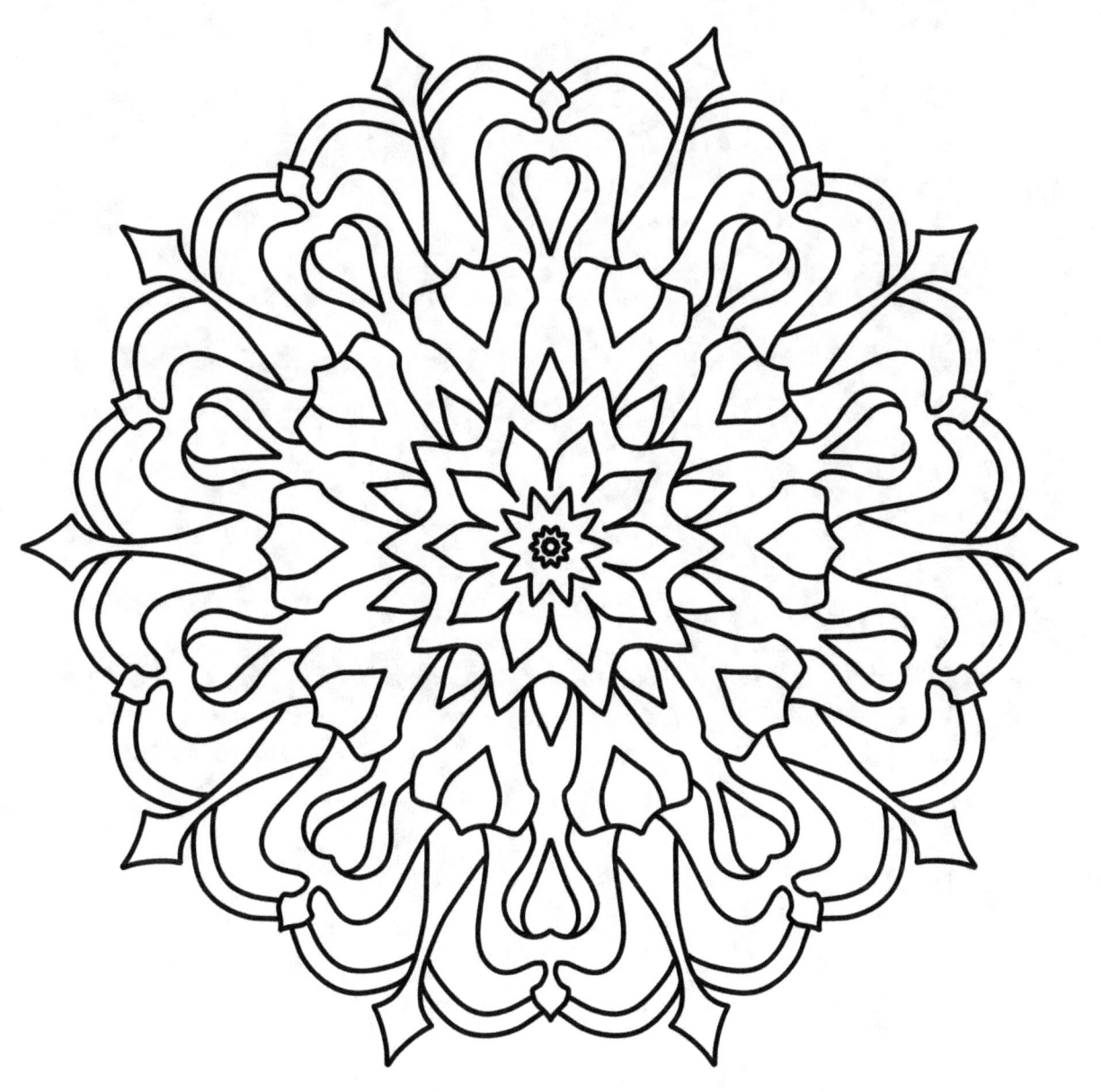

BOO-ME-RANG! BOO-ME-RANG!

Mandala level: Apprentice

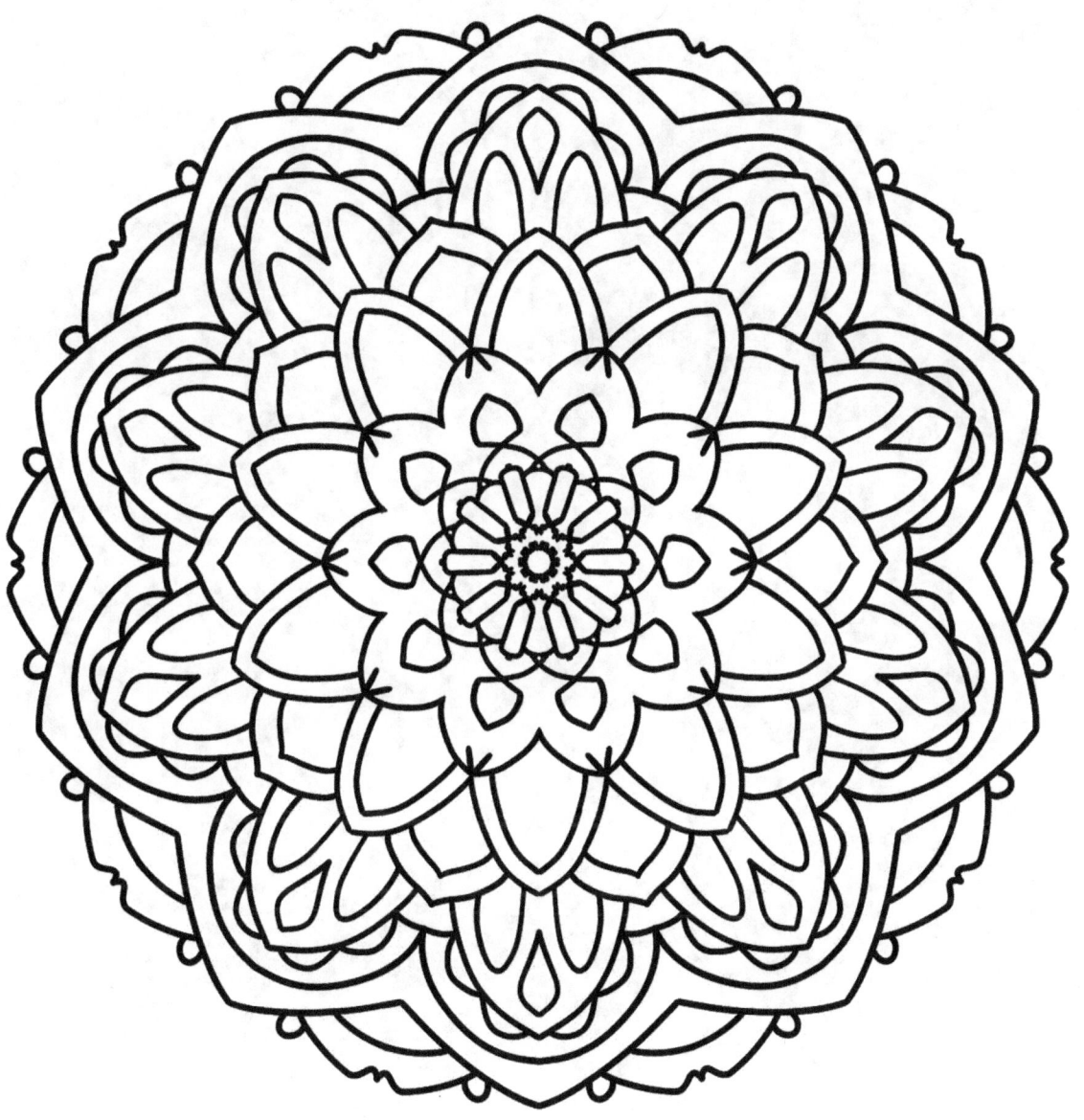

Just kidding. Please don't throw me... Actually don't throw anything, ever.

Mandala level: Apprentice

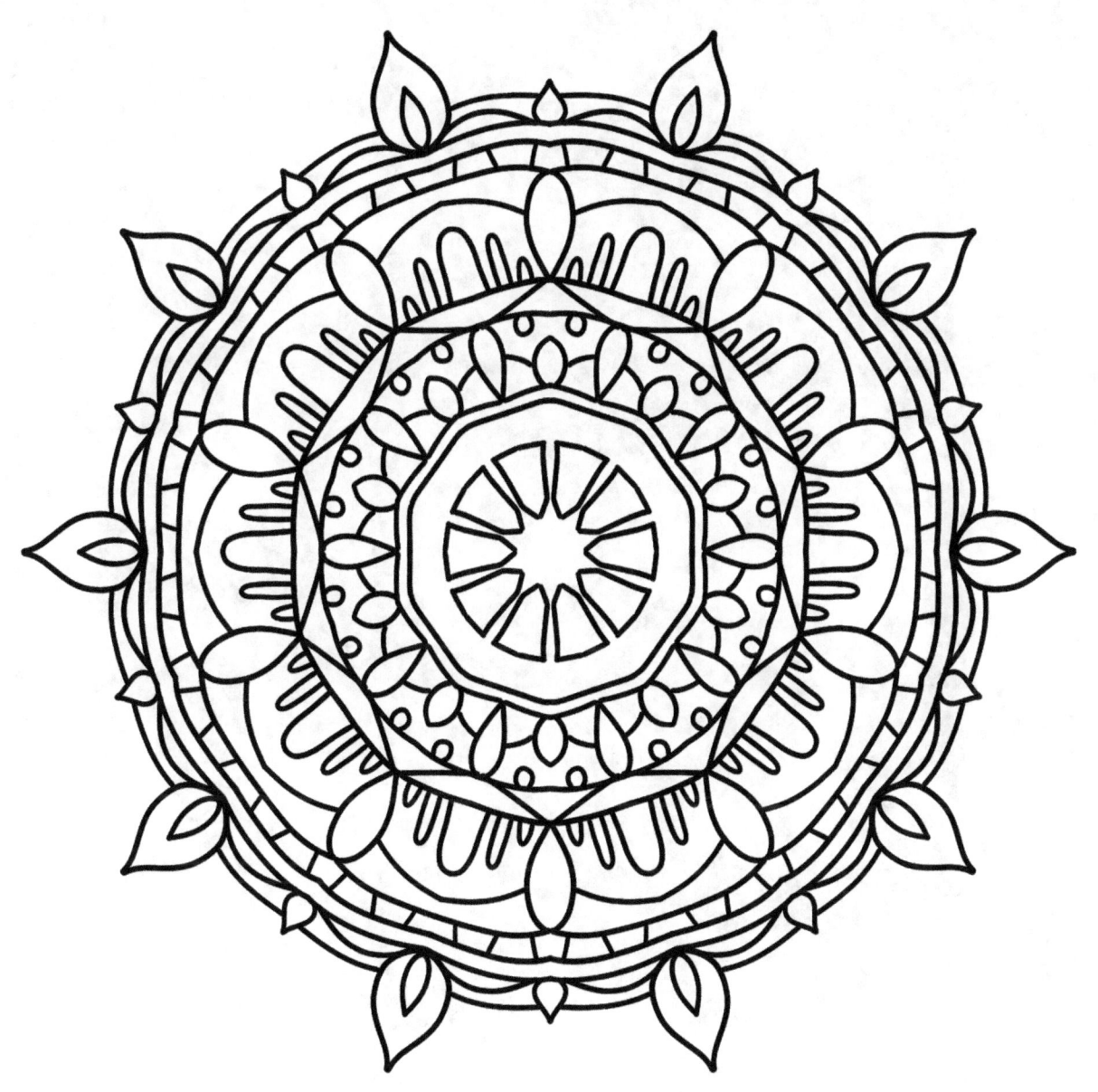

Unless you practice some sort of sport that involves throwing.

Mandala level: Intermediate

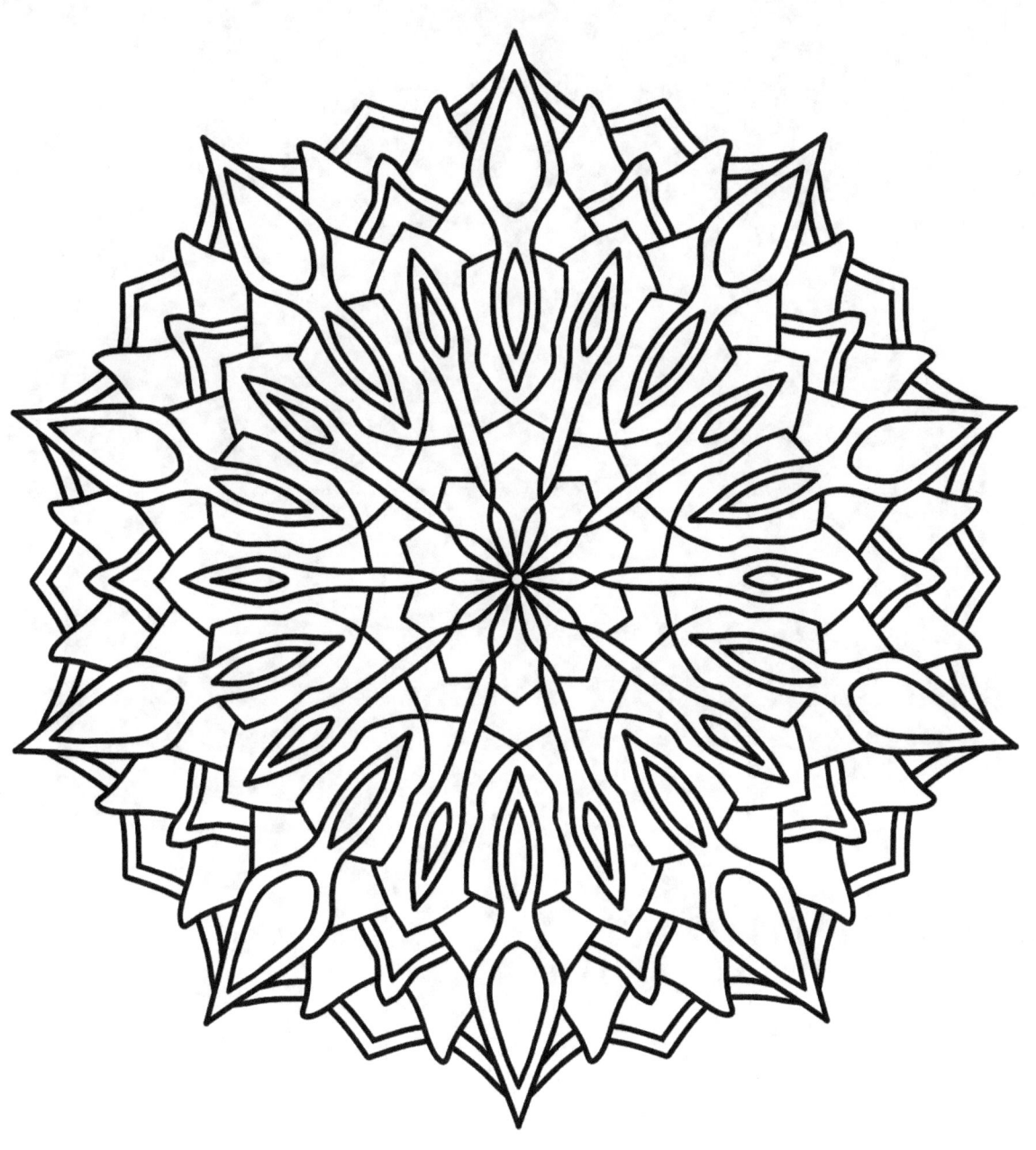

**Try to imagine a color that doesn't exist.
Exactly, you can't. Now, go impress your friends.**

Mandala level: Intermediate

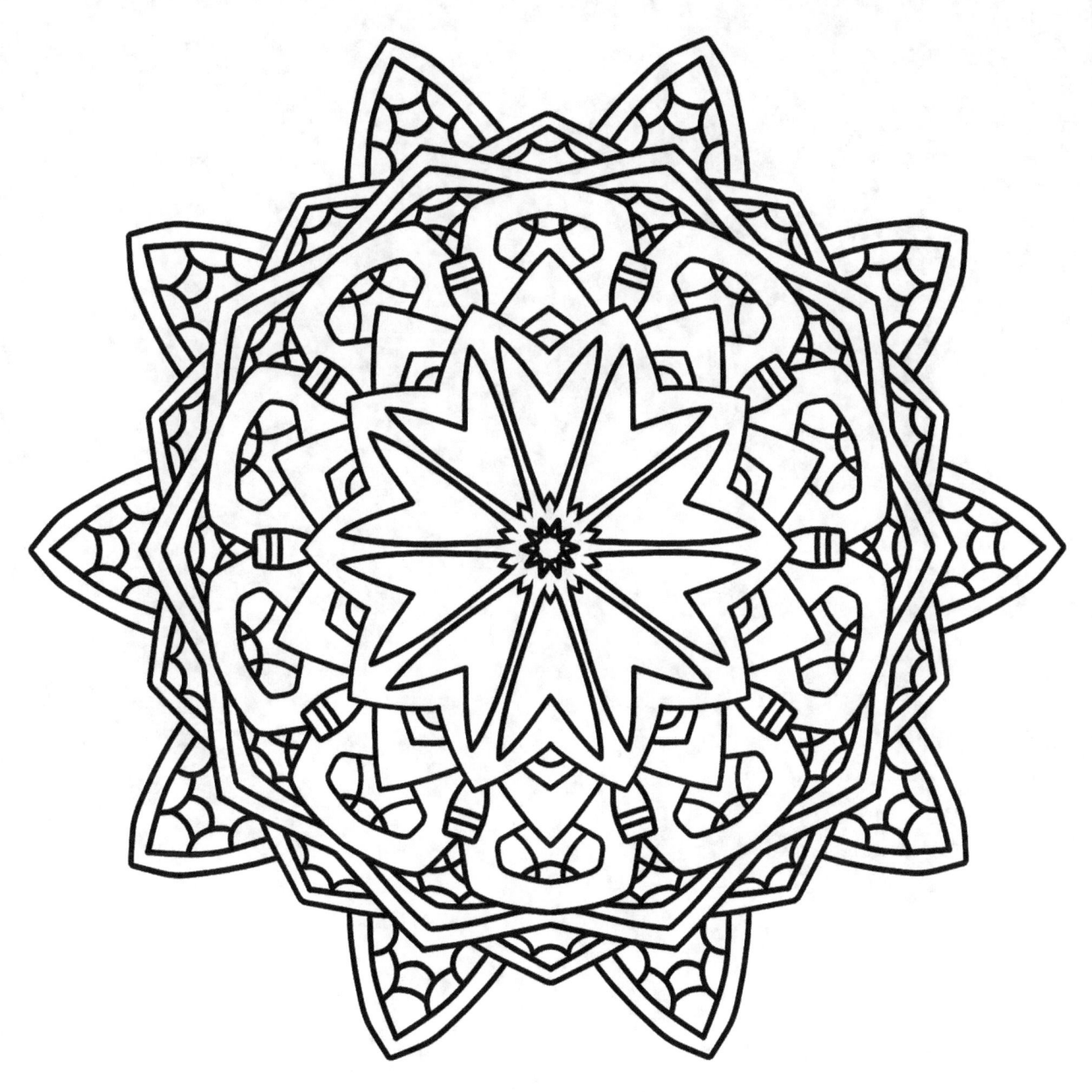

By the way, don't ever let anyone tell you that you can't do anything! I believe in you.

Mandala level: Intermediate

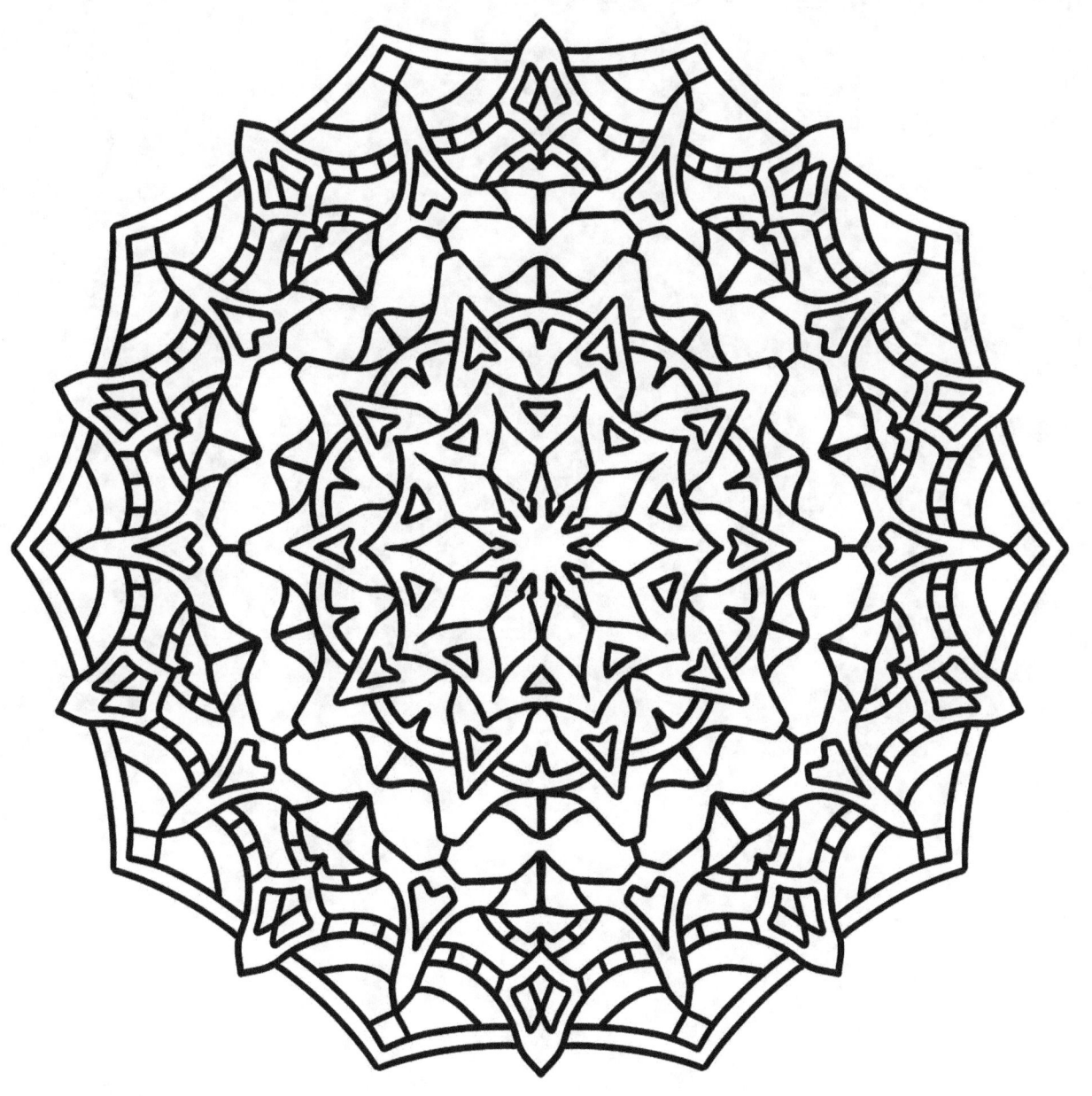

Unless you're trying to imagine a color that doesn't exist. Nobody can do that.

Mandala level: Intermediate

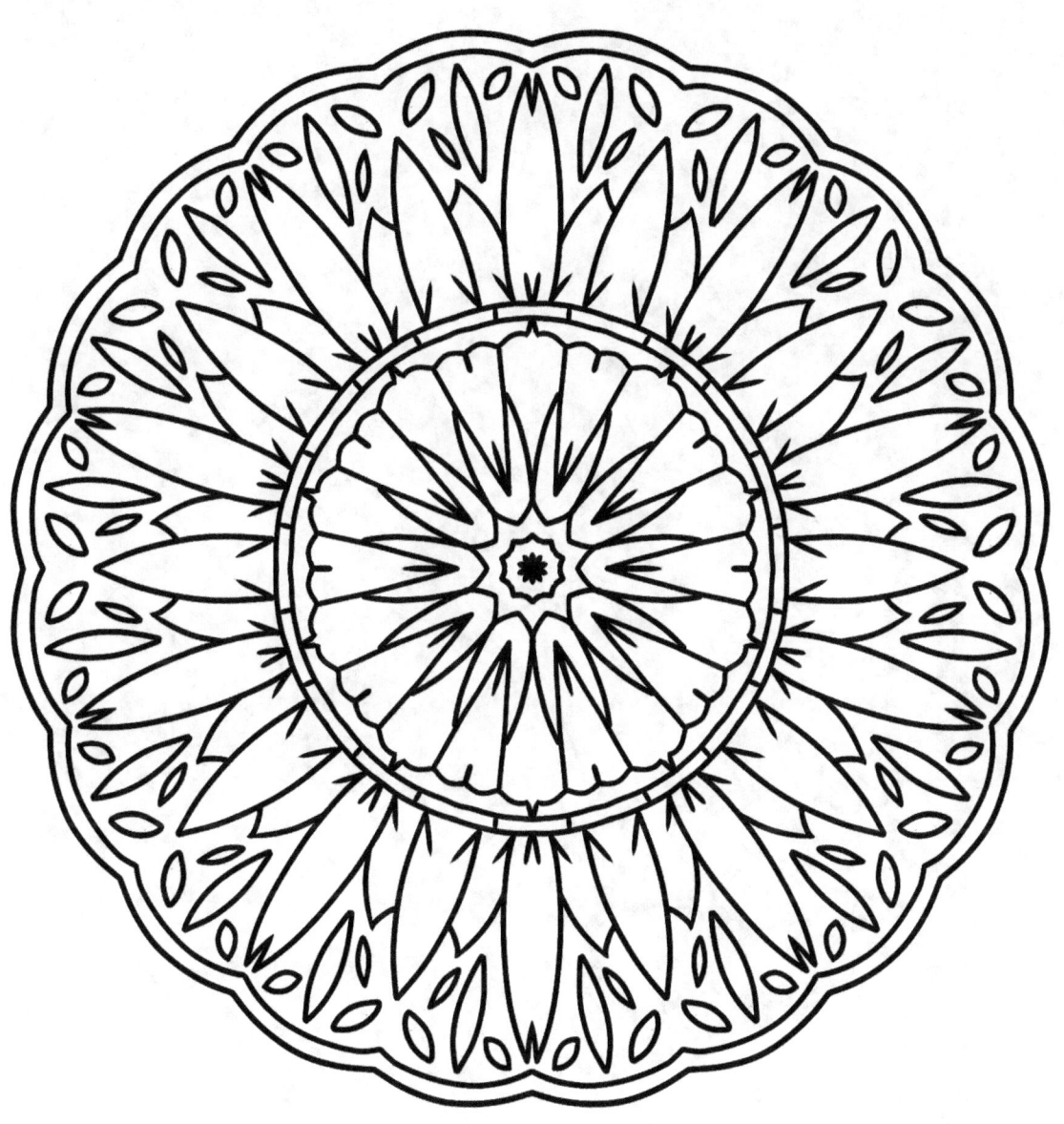

Riddle time:
If a bear walks a mile south, a mile east, then a mile north back to where it started...
Who's not coloring the mandala? You.

Mandala level: Intermediate

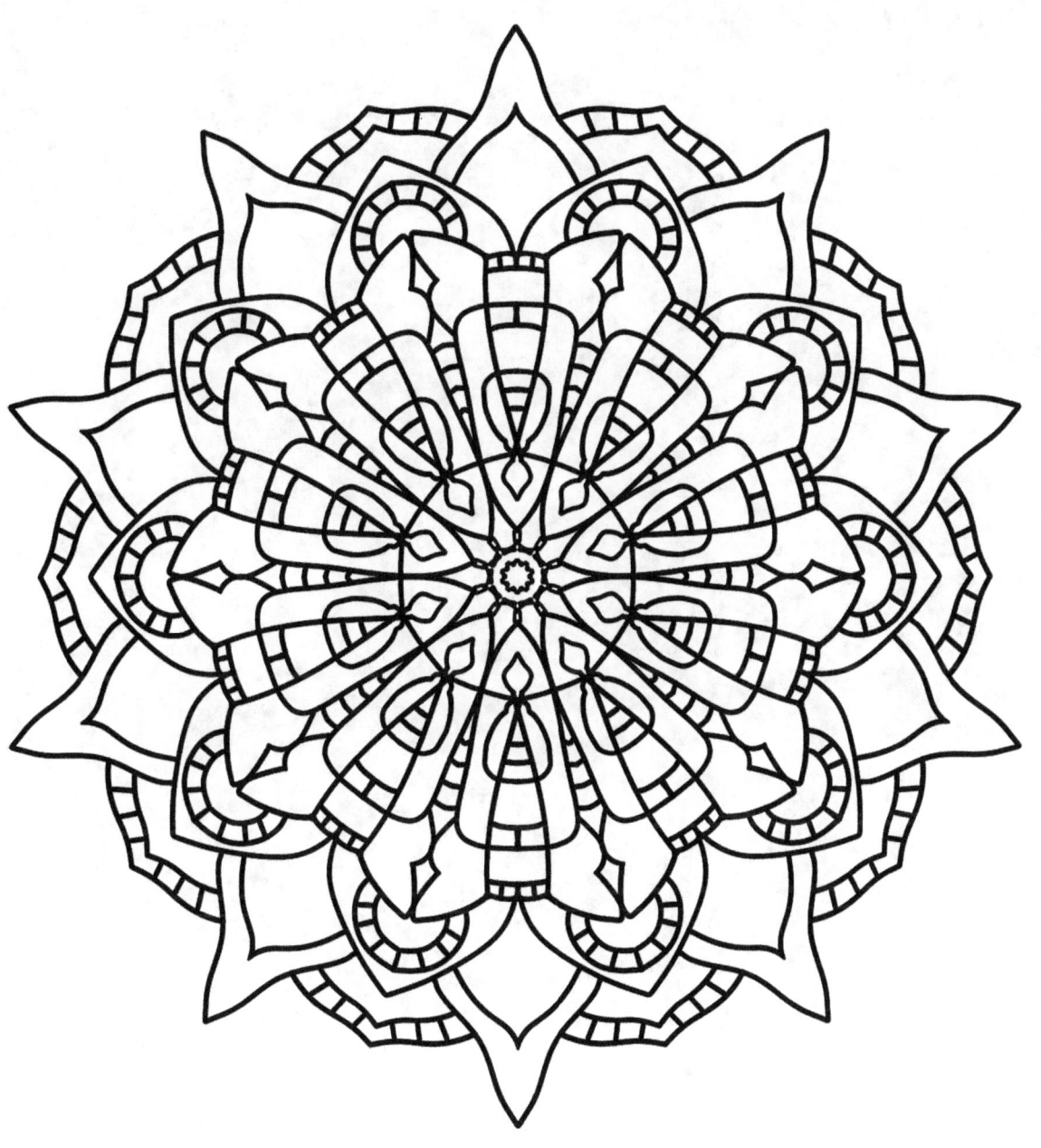

I want you to color the following mandala as if I was going to pay you.

Mandala level: Intermediate

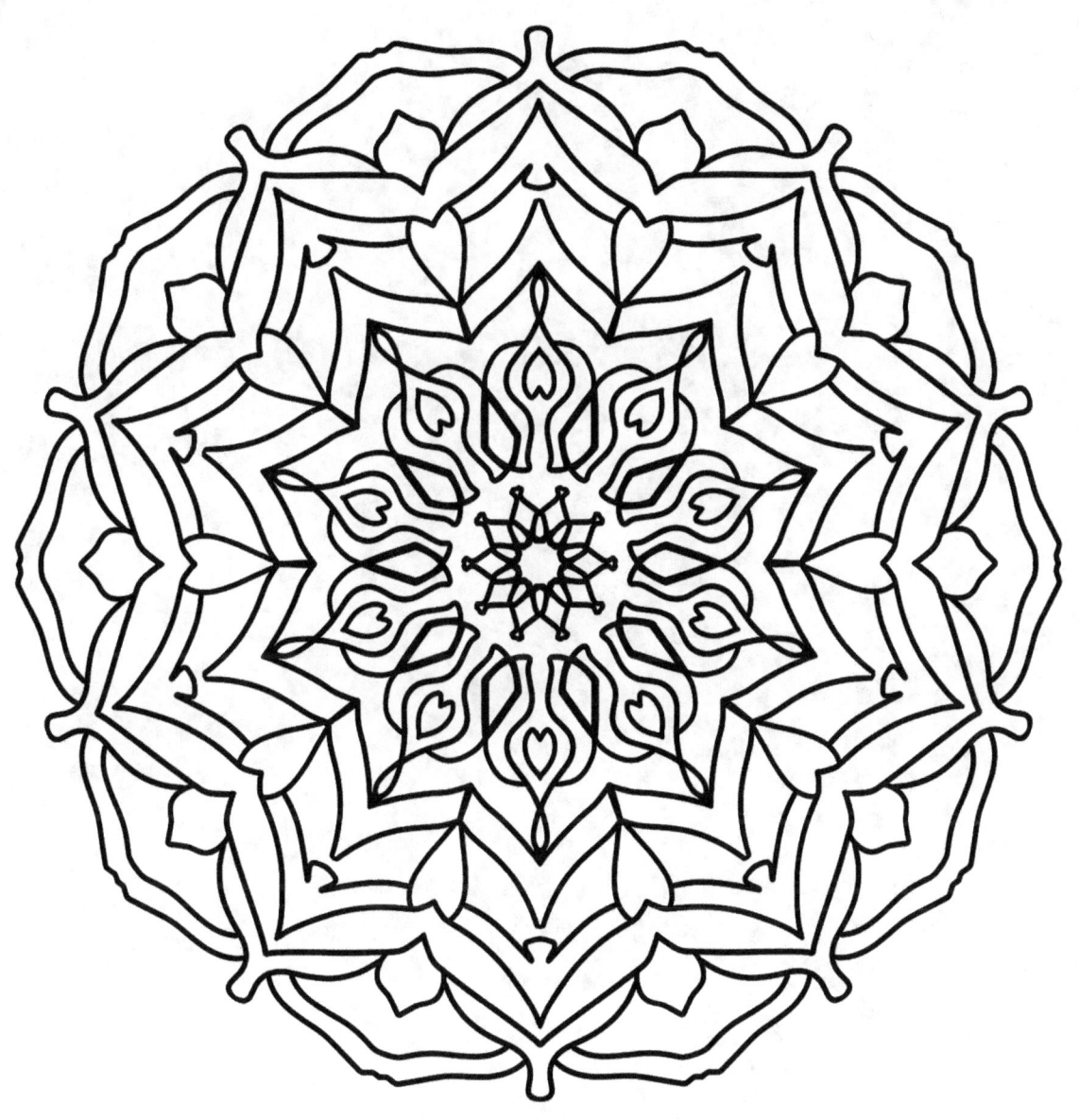

I just wanted to remind you that everything you do to me is permanent; so you better do it right on your first try, because you have one chance. ONE. CHANCE. ONLY. Make it count. Now let's have some fun!

Mandala level: Intermediate

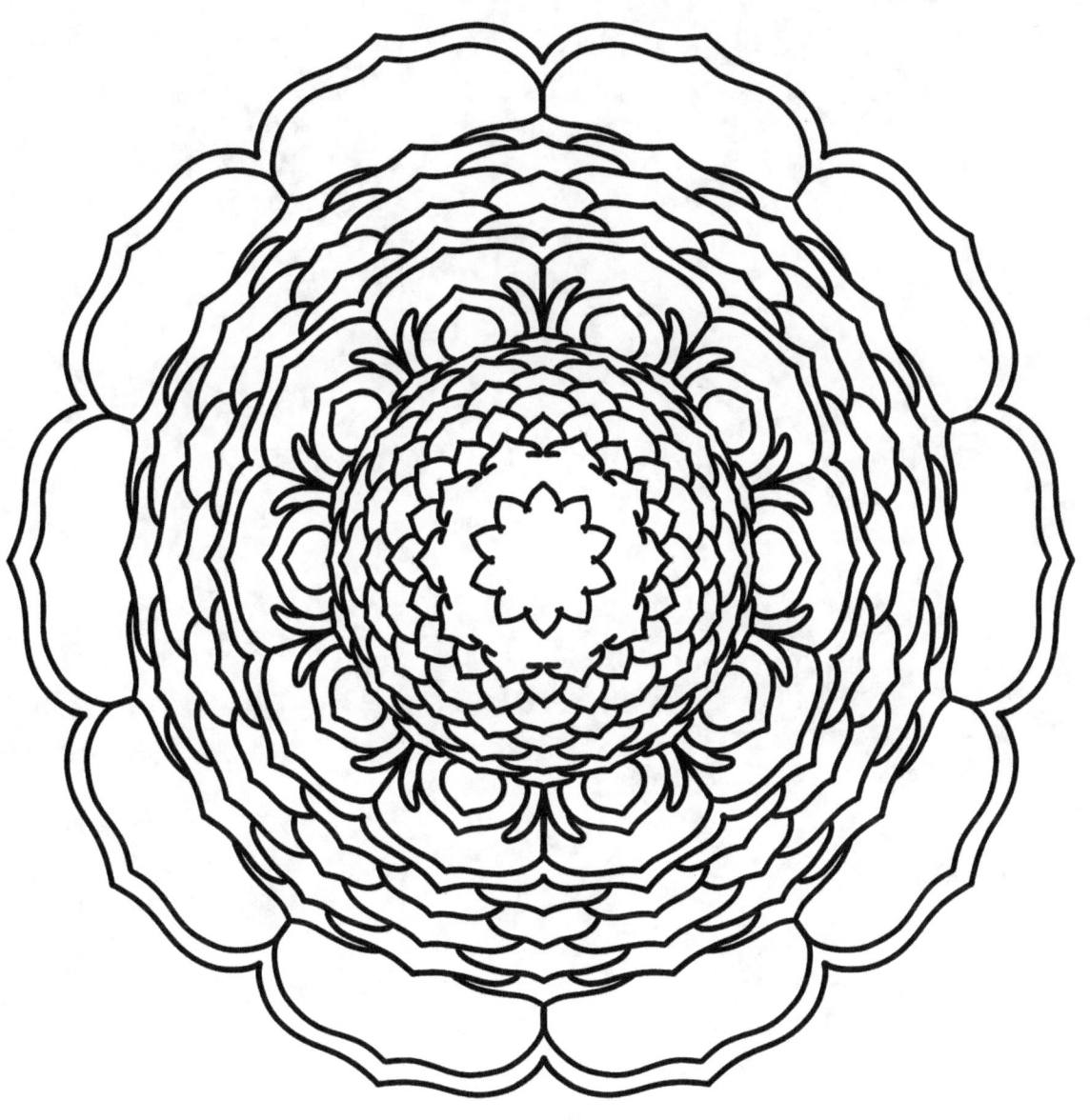

Am I distracting you? Do you want me to leave? Okay.

Mandala level: Intermediate

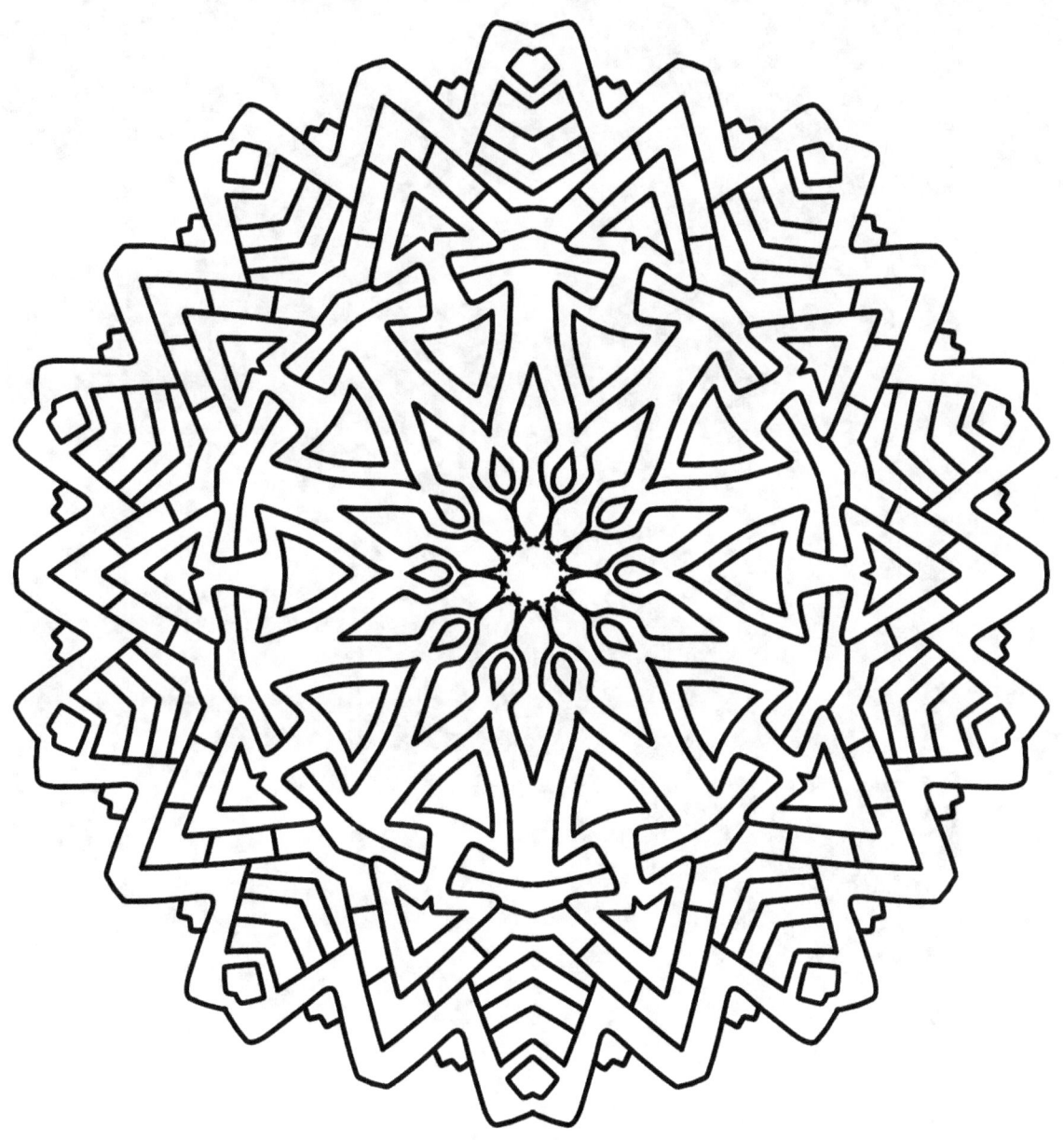

Mandala level: Intermediate

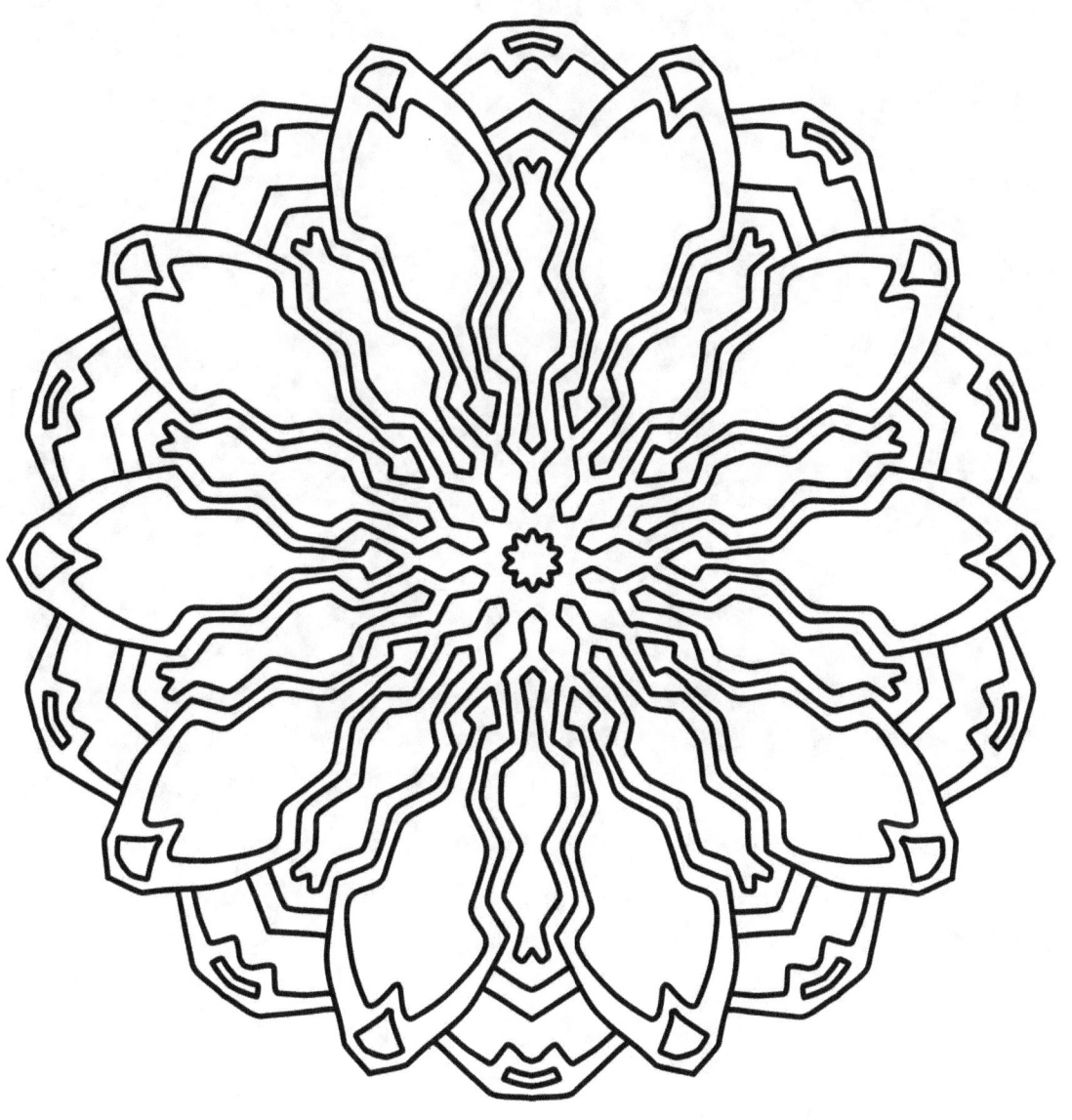

**Don't worry, I didn't go anywhere.
I just wanted to teach you to be careful with what you wish for.**

Mandala level: Intermediate

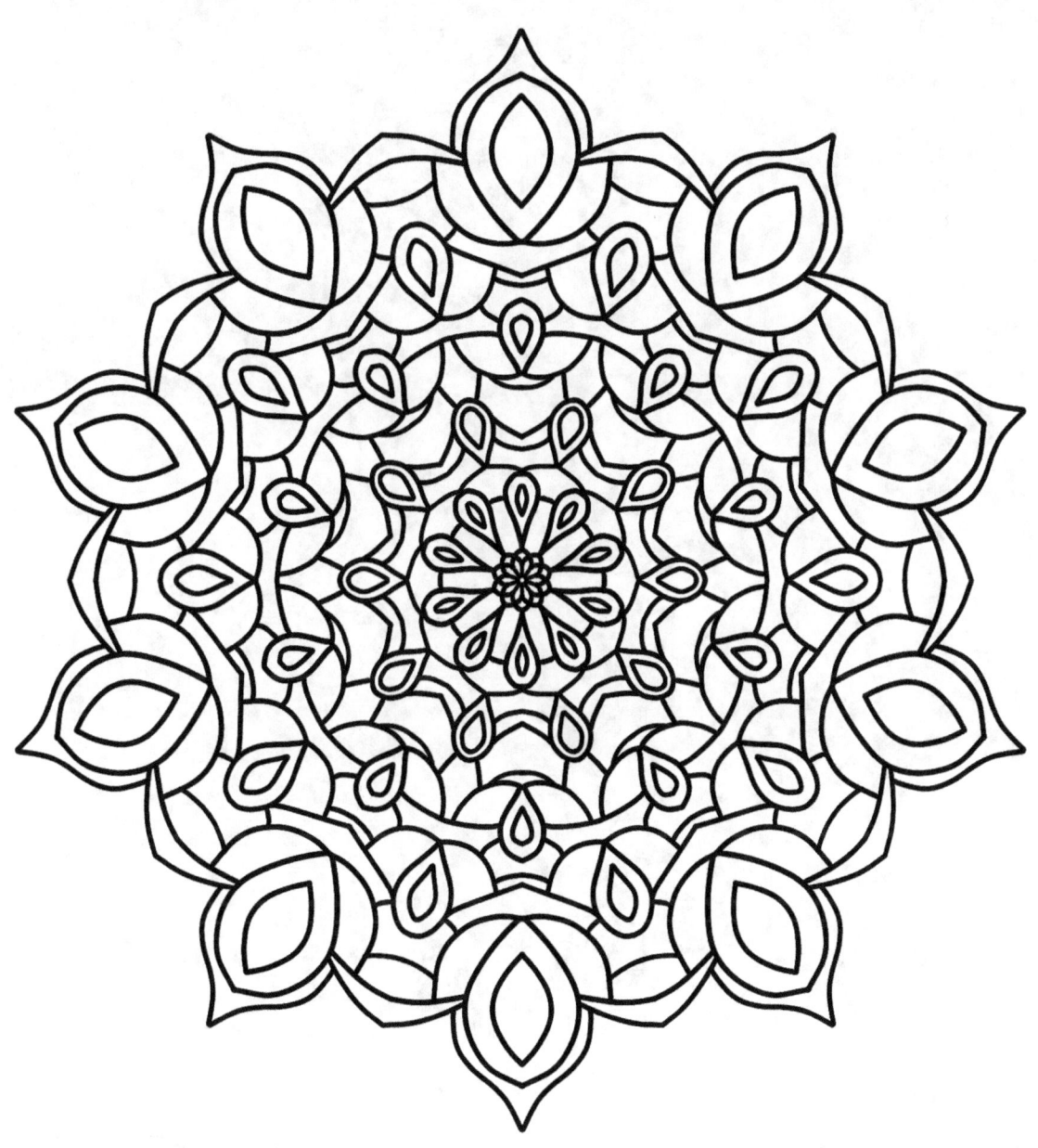

Even though the last mandala ended up terrible, I know you are doing your best and THAT'S what makes you an artist.

Mandala level: Intermediate

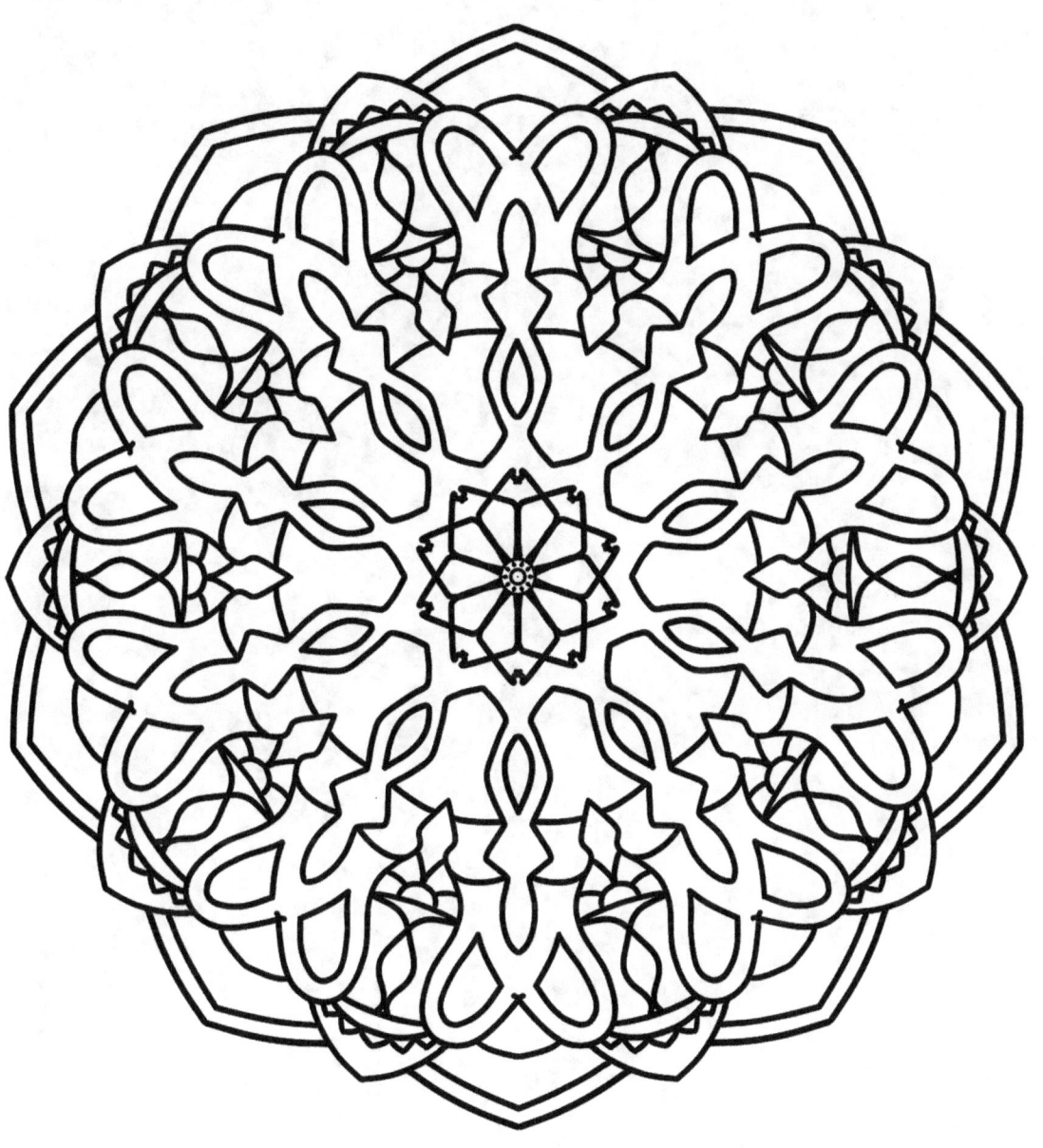

Did you know there are approximately 10,988 teeth in a whale's mouth?

Mandala level: Intermediate

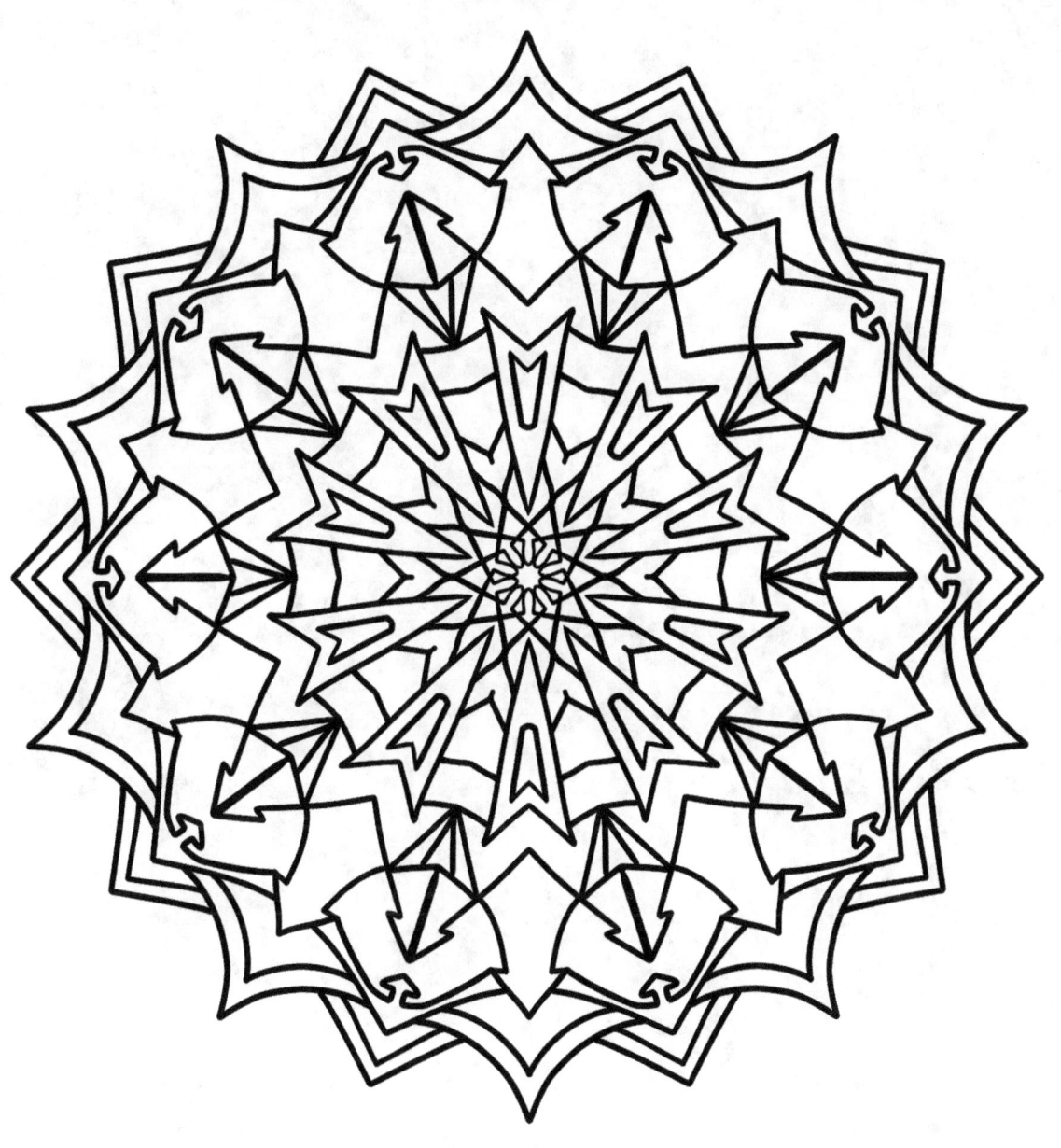

Just kidding. Whales don't even have teeth.

Mandala level: Advanced

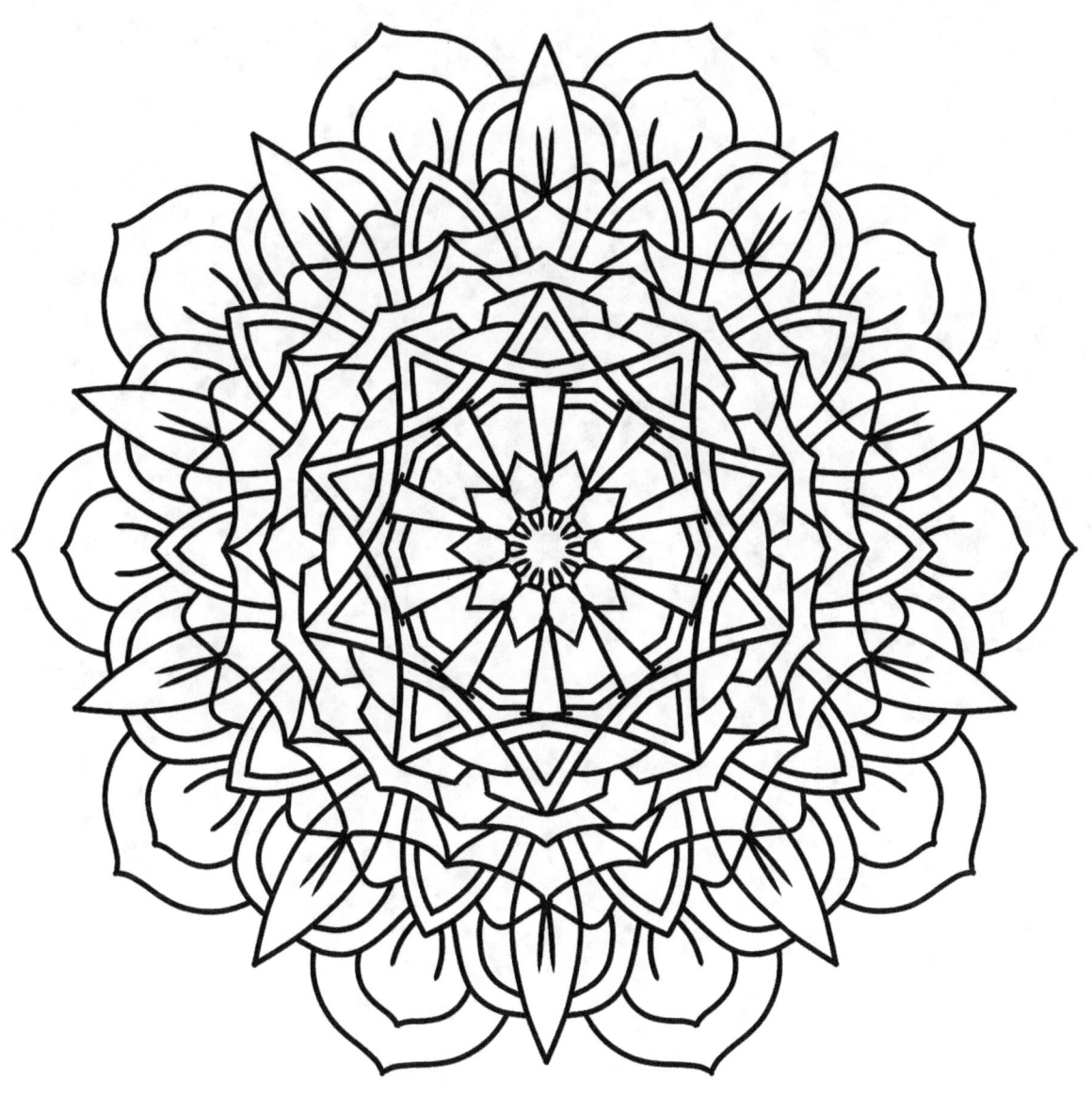

Learn not to trust everything you read in a book.

Mandala level: Advanced

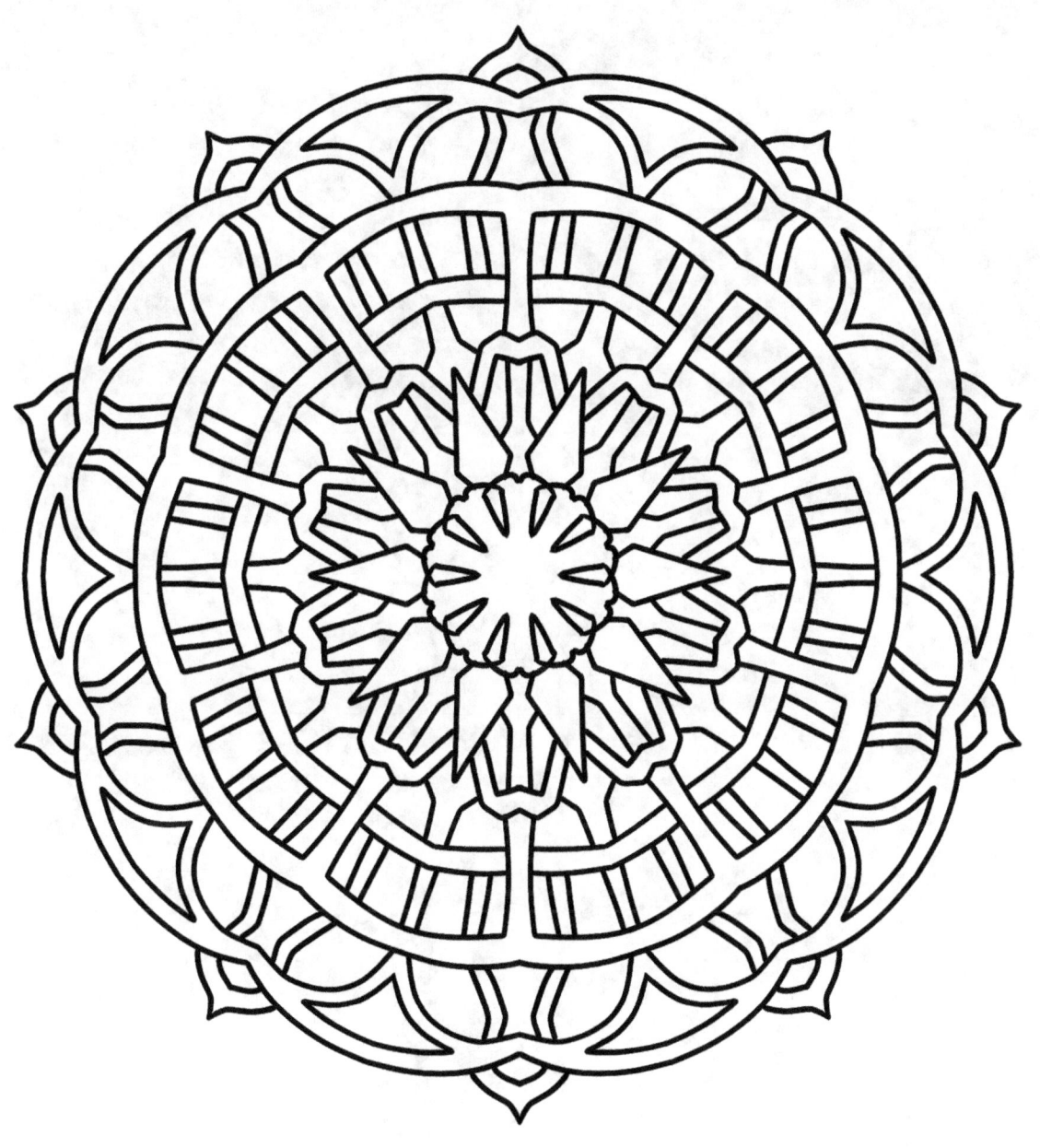

I guess it's nice spending time with you.

Mandala level: Advanced

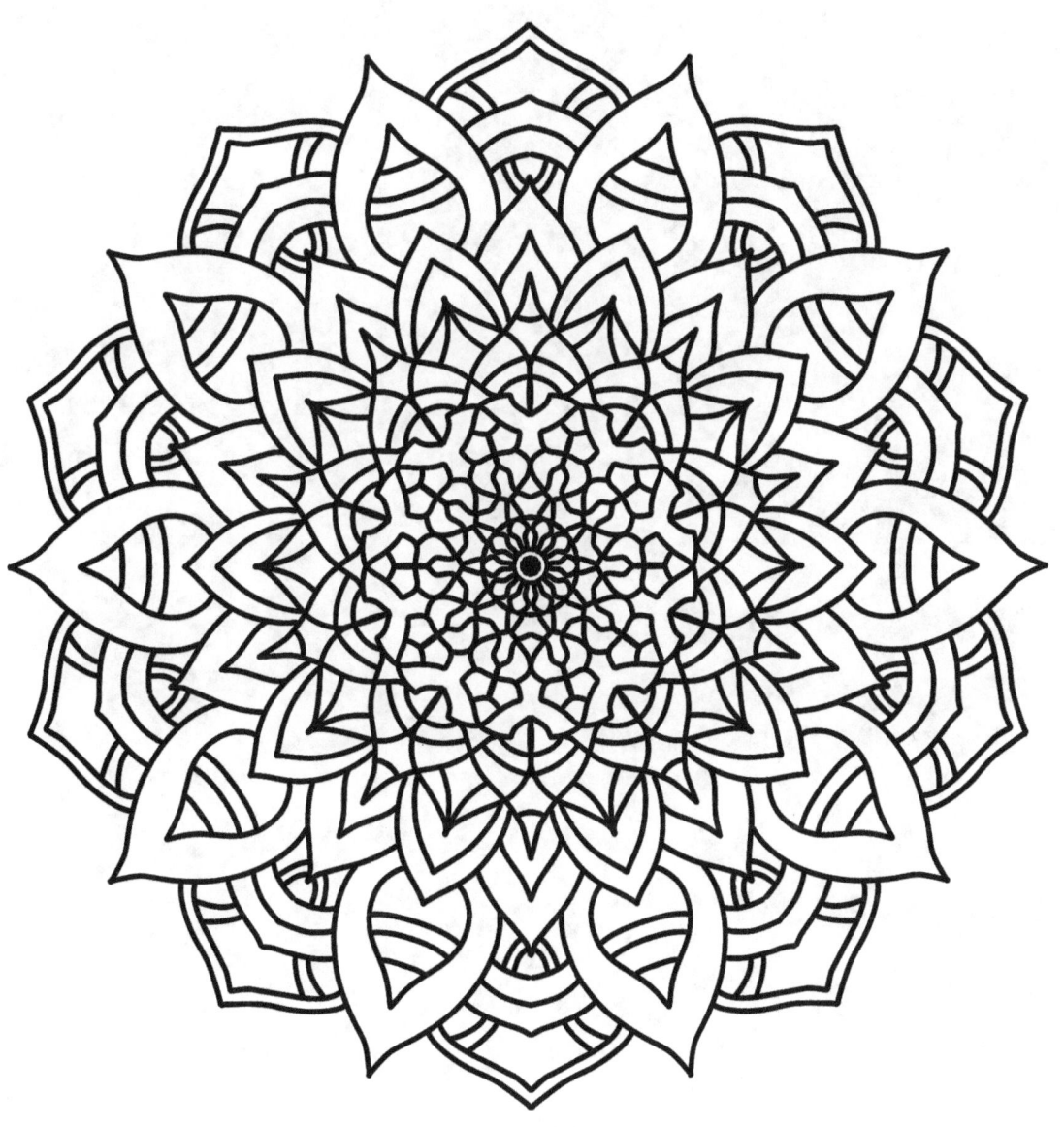

Look at this mandala. I made this. Just for you. Enjoy.

Mandala level: Advanced

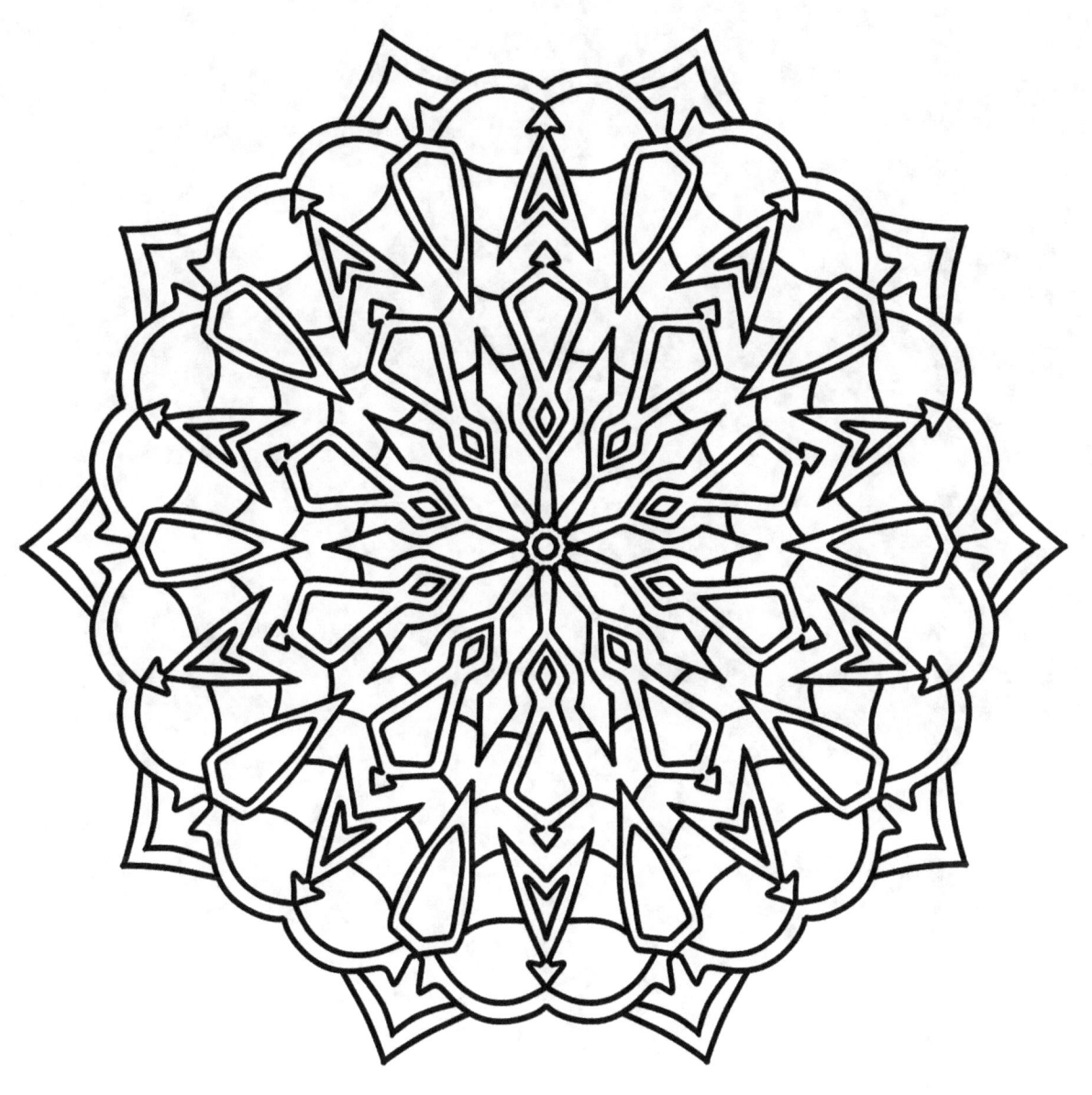

That's okay. There's no need to get emotional.

Mandala level: Advanced

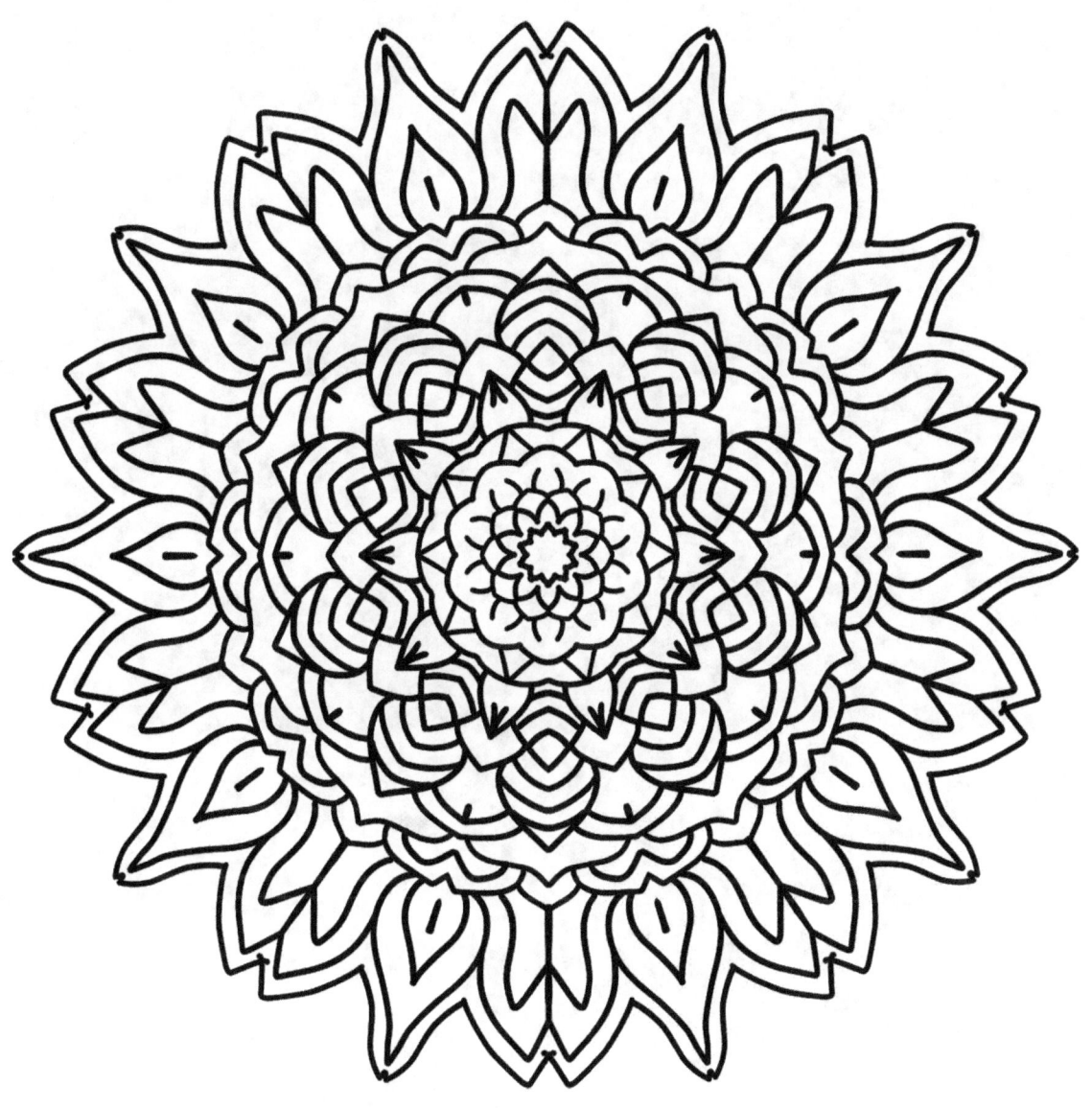

**Remember the surprise I mentioned earlier?
Well, there was none.
Never expect anything and you'll never be disappointed.**

Mandala level: Advanced

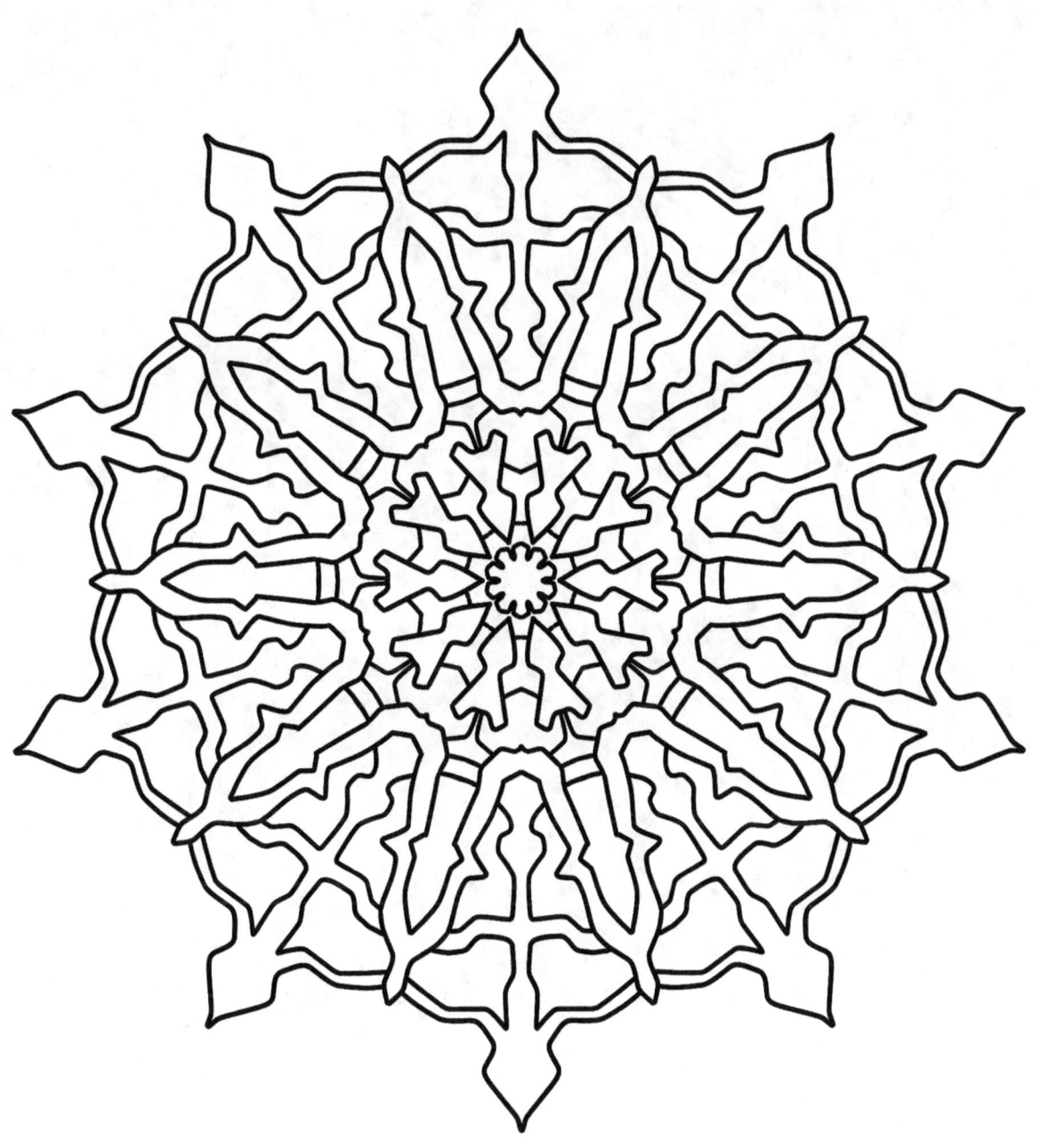

Before being a mandala book, I used to be a scuba diver.

Mandala level: Advanced

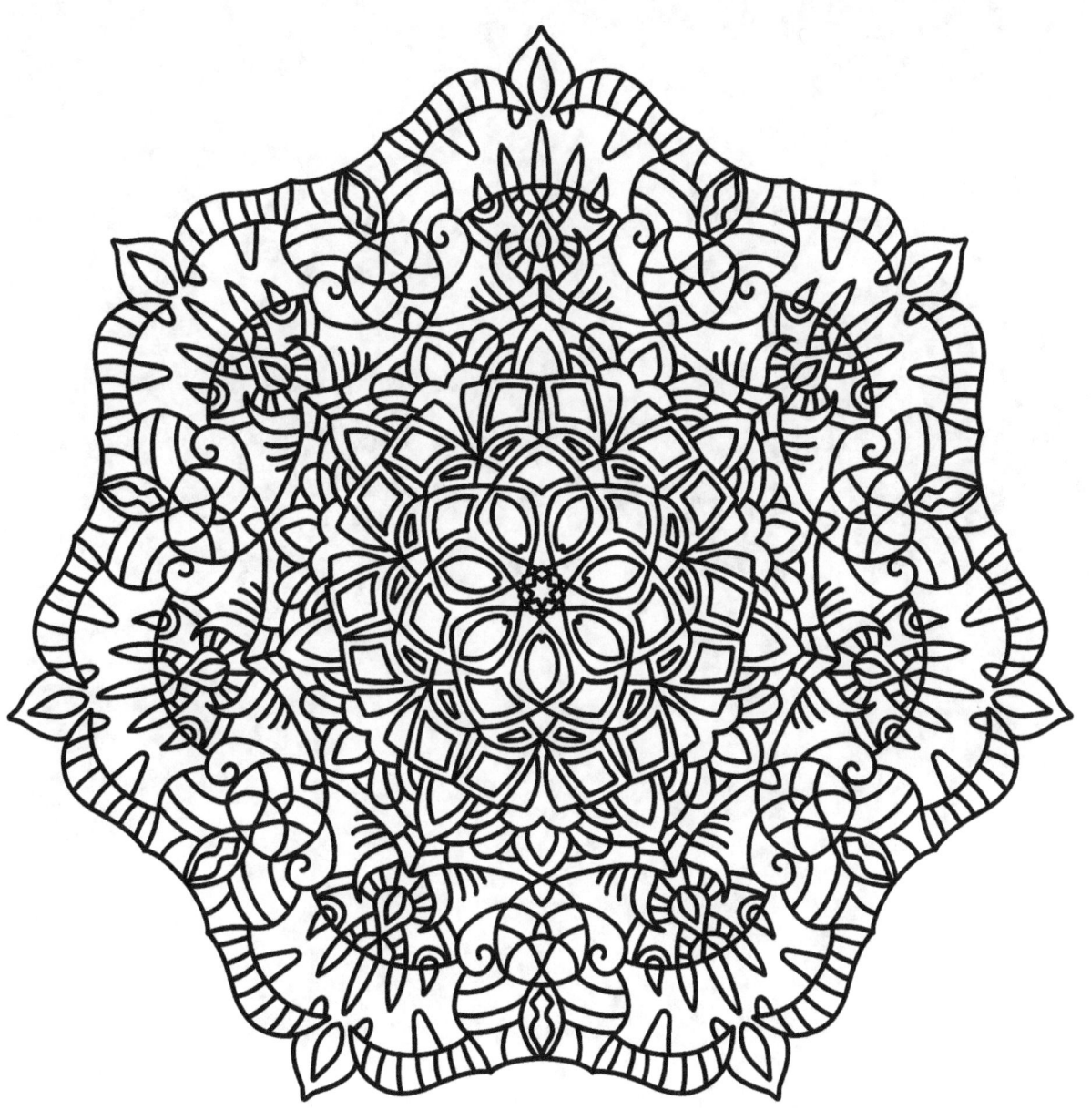

That's how I learned that one thing about whales.

Mandala level: Advanced

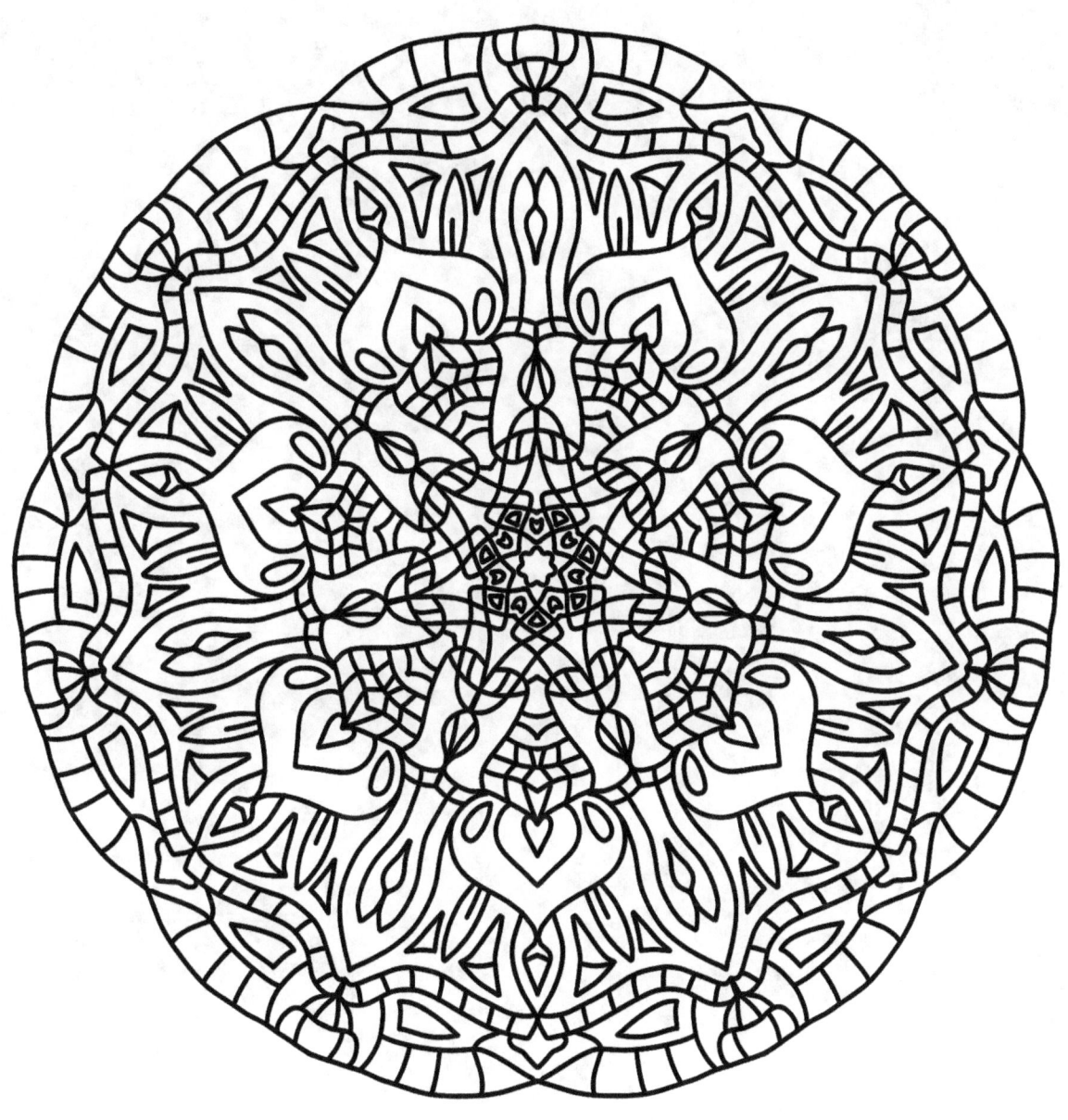

We are reaching the end. I can see the light from here.

Mandala level: Advanced

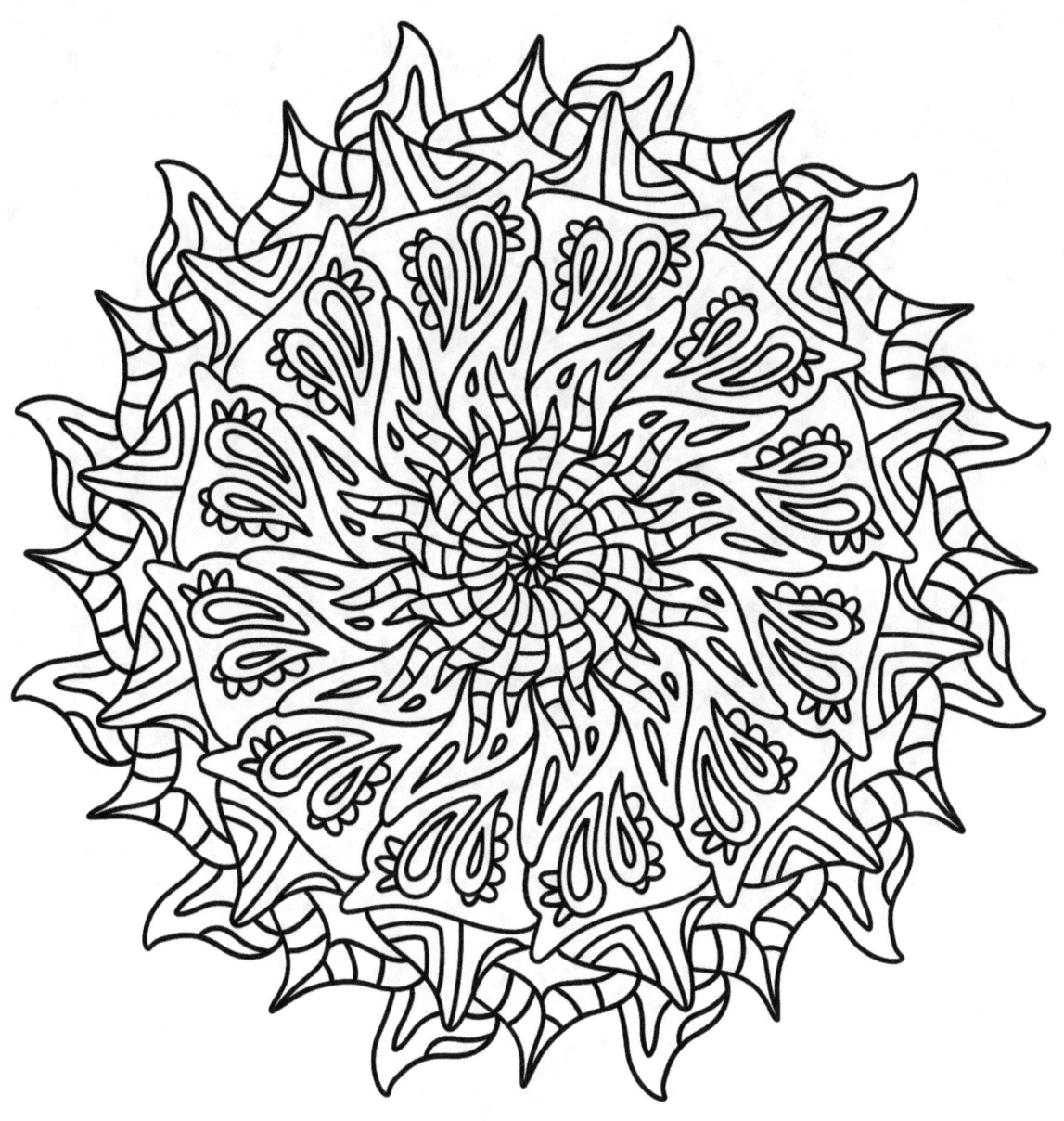

This is the longest relationship I've ever had.

Mandala level: Advanced

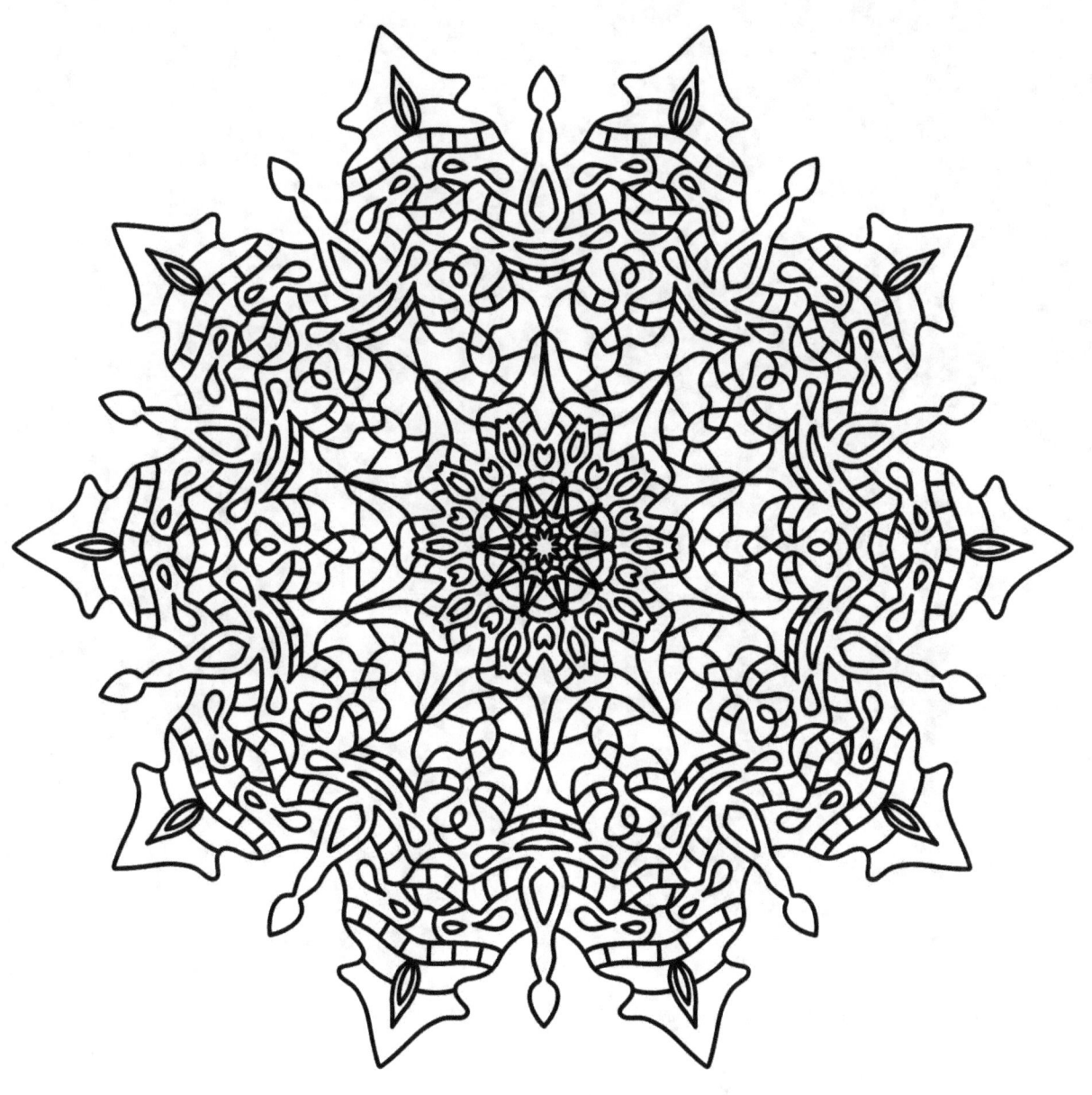

I don't tell this to anyone, but you are my favorite person, so far.

Mandala level: Advanced

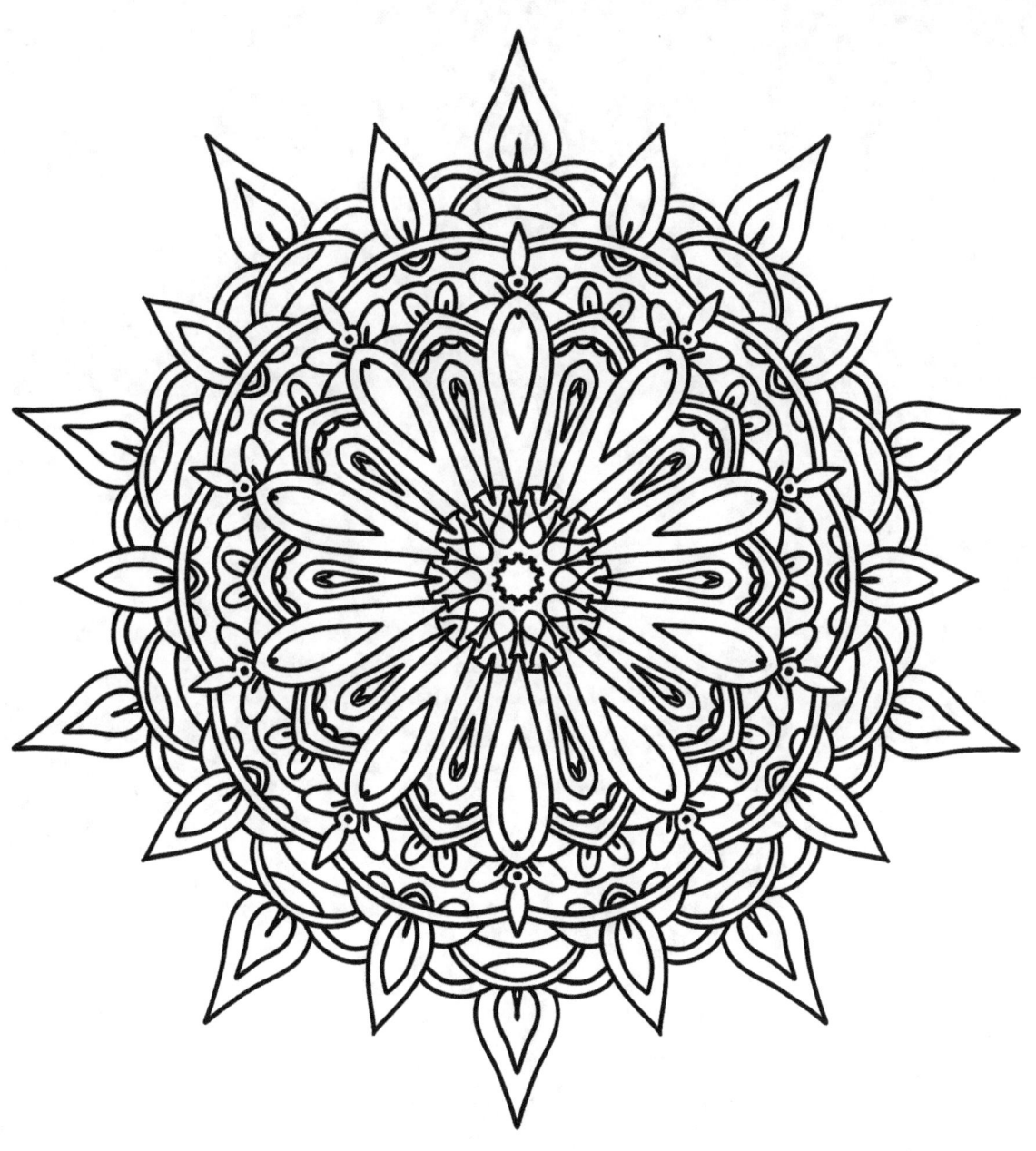

Each time you color me, a part of you stays with me forever. I hope it goes both ways...
Maybe you should tattoo my name somewhere, just to be sure.

Mandala level: Advanced

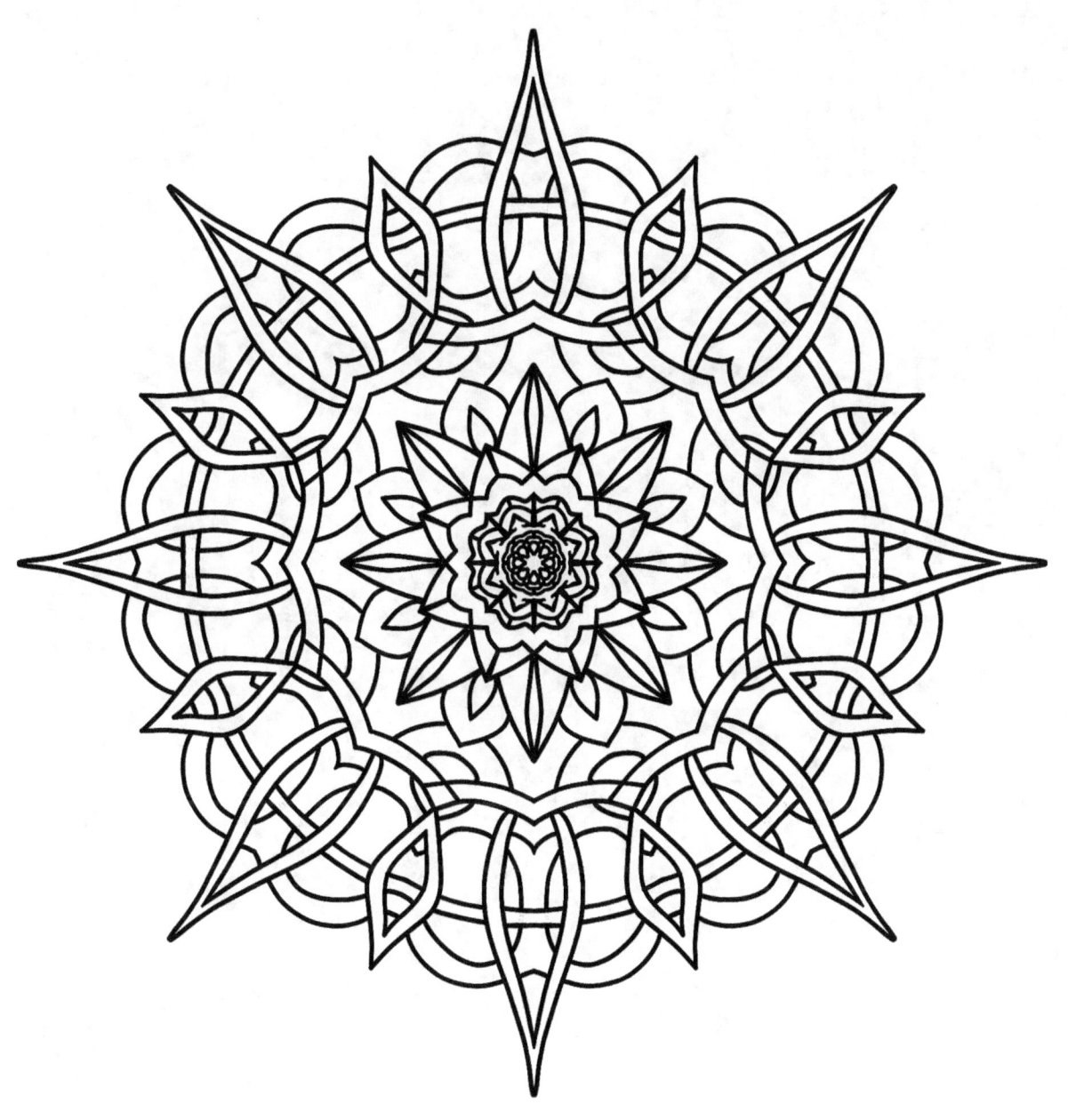

Maybe I'll come back... Or maybe I'll go back to scuba diving. Who knows?

Mandala level: Advanced

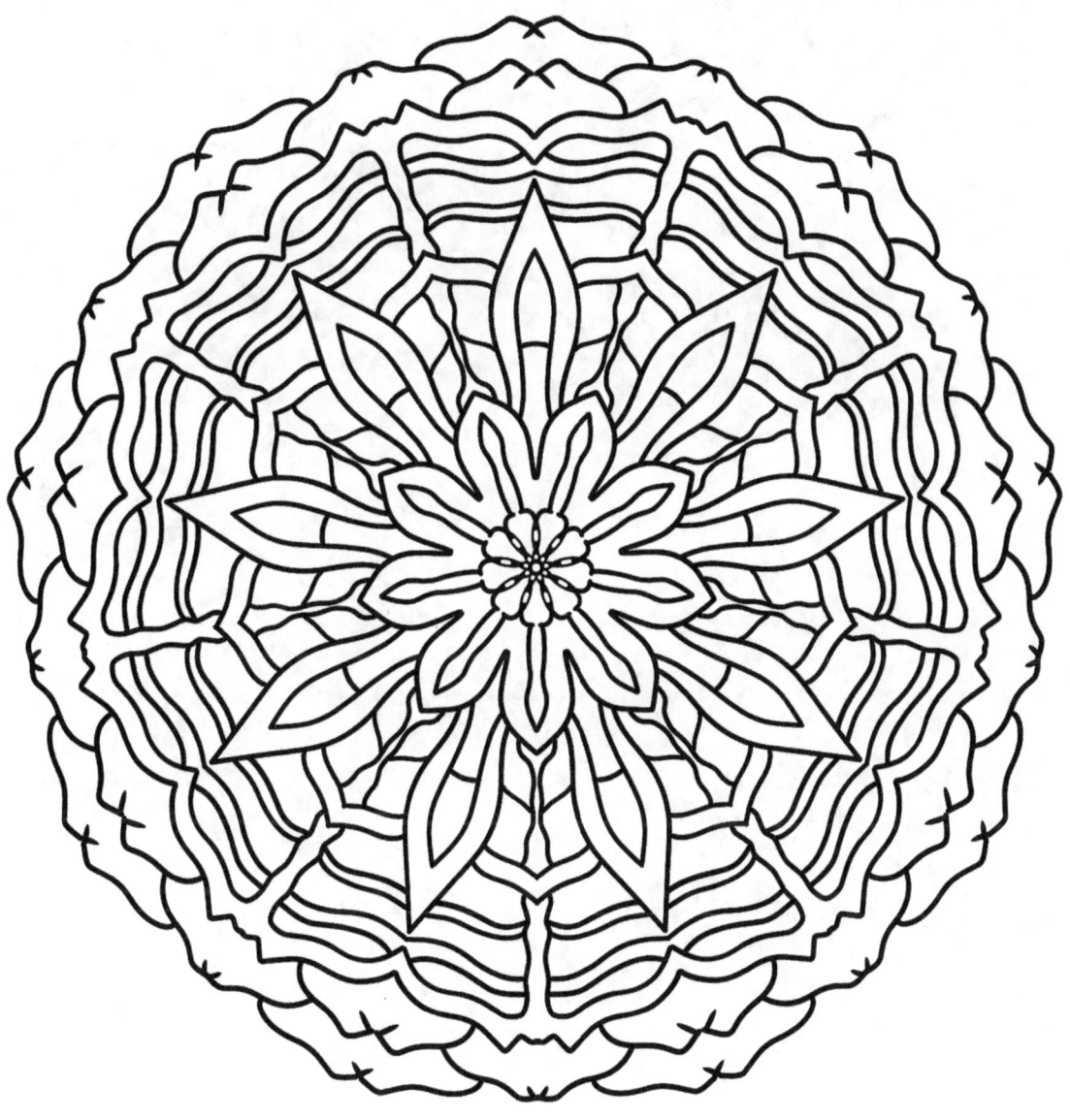

**Perhaps I should try hiking. Do you like hiking?
I'd appreciate it if you took me for a hike.**

Mandala level: Almost there

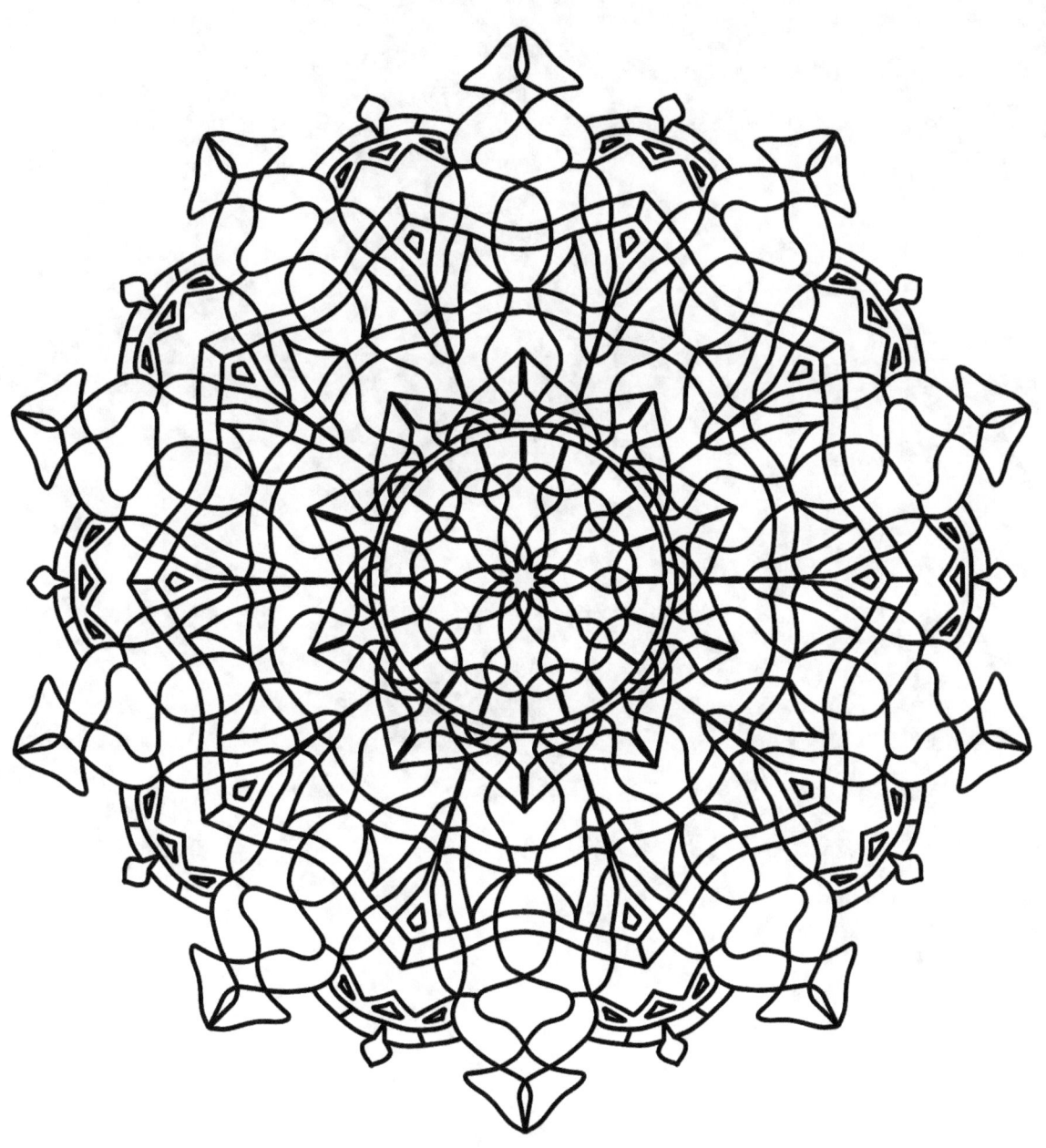

Not as a date, I mean, you can tell more people if you want.

Mandala level: Almost there

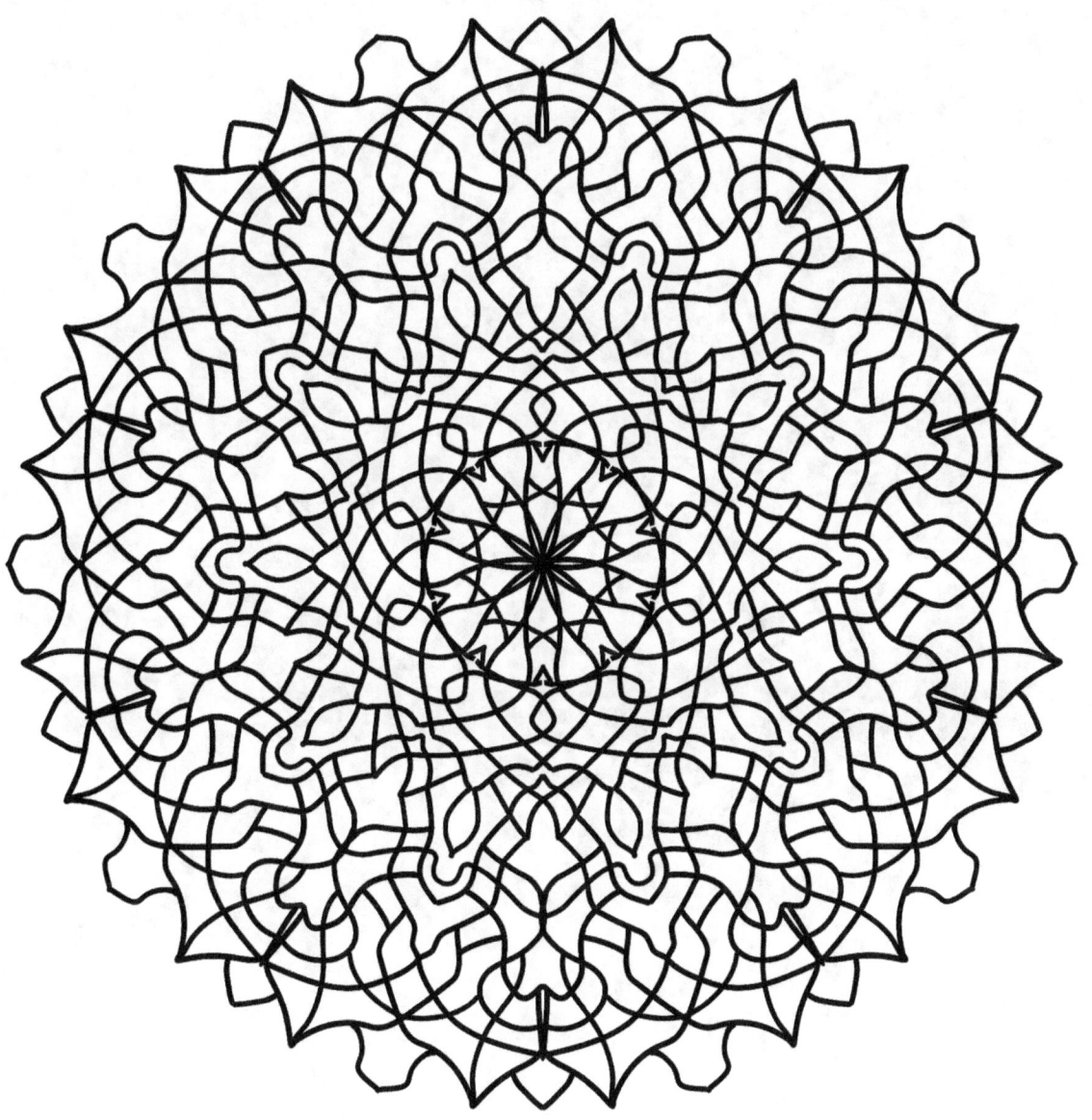

I would say I hate goodbyes. But I don't.

Mandala level: Almost there

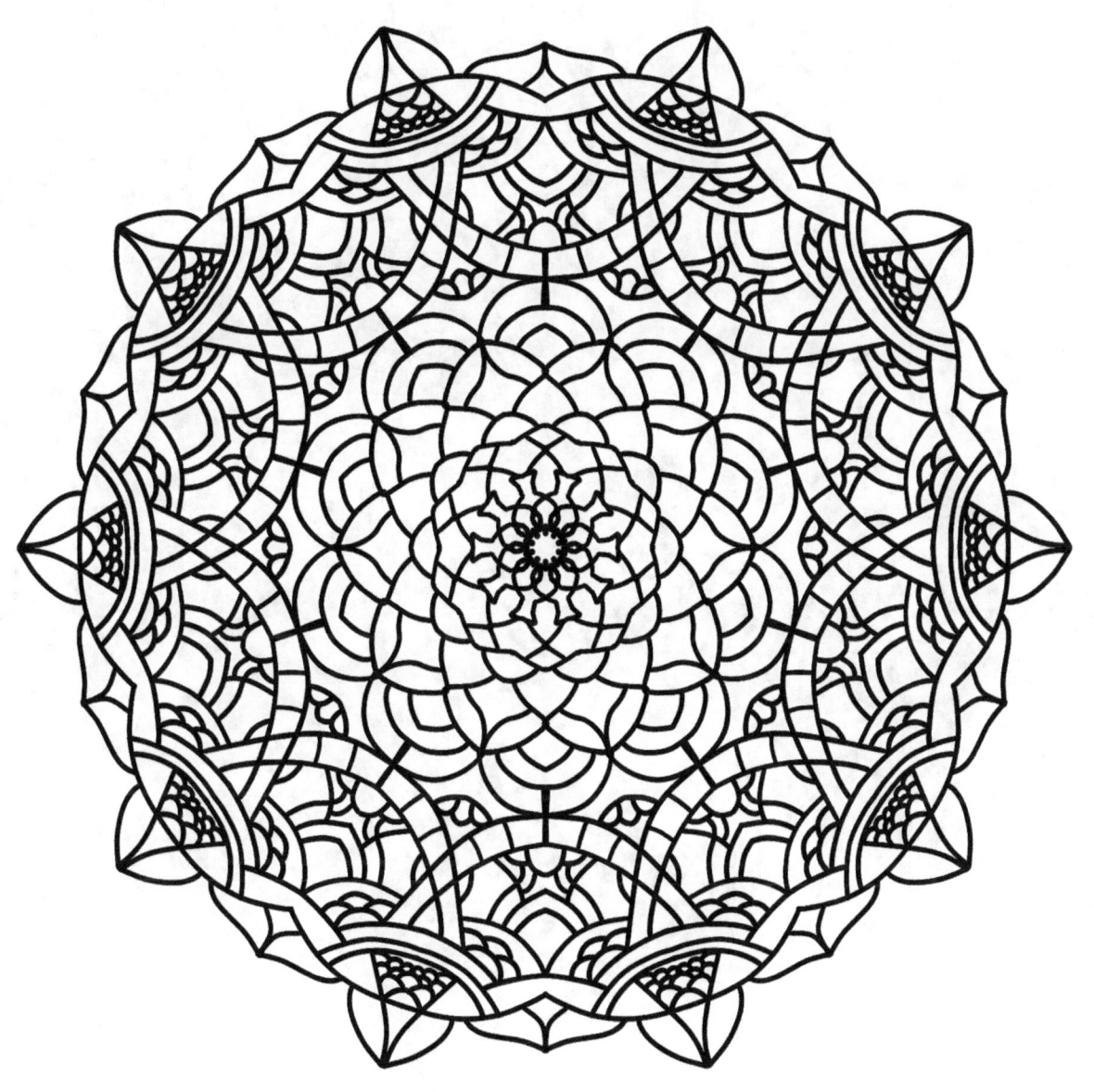

But I got a soft spot for you. I like you.

Mandala level: Almost there

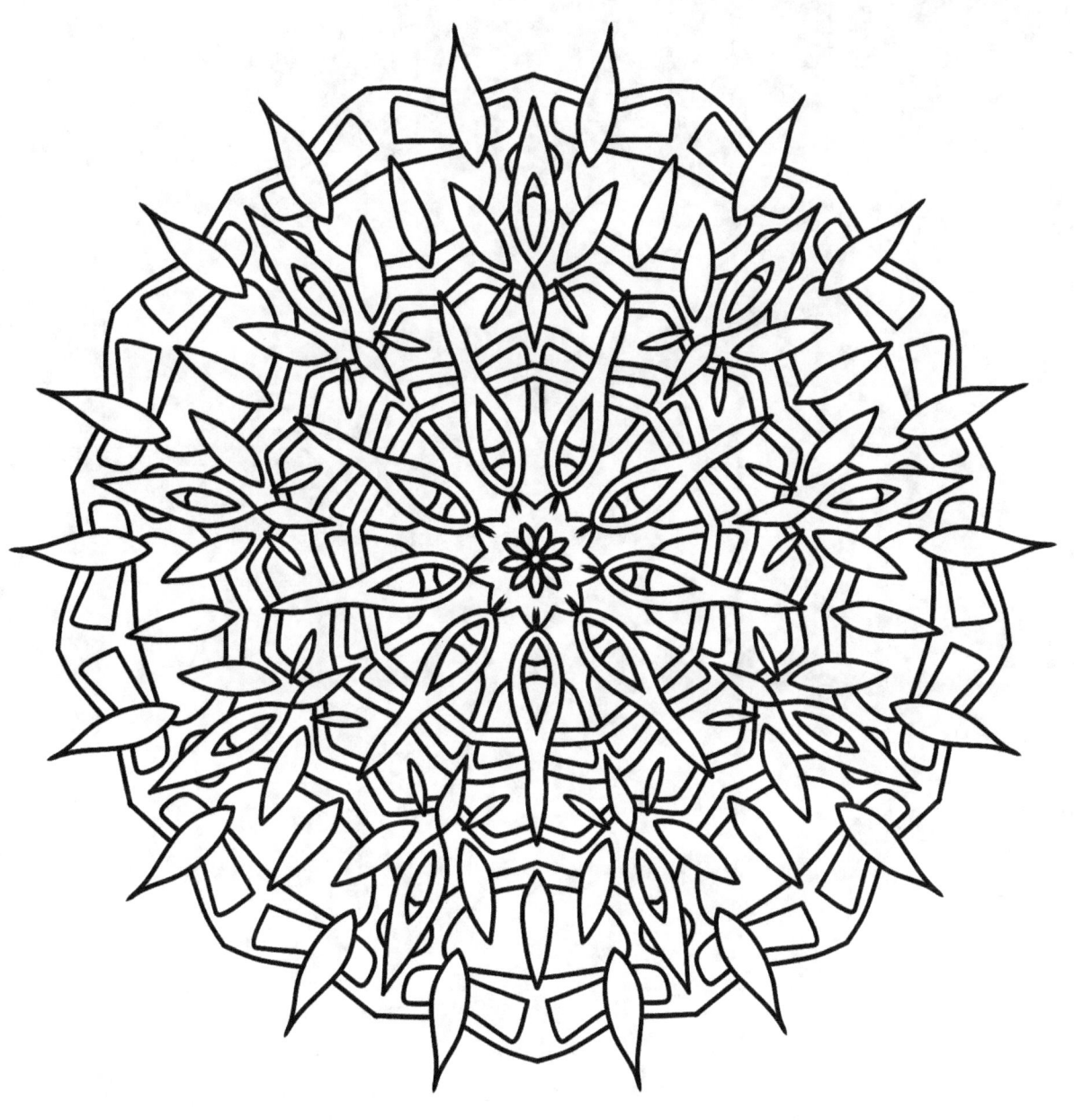

Remember me when you get famous.

Mandala level: Almost there

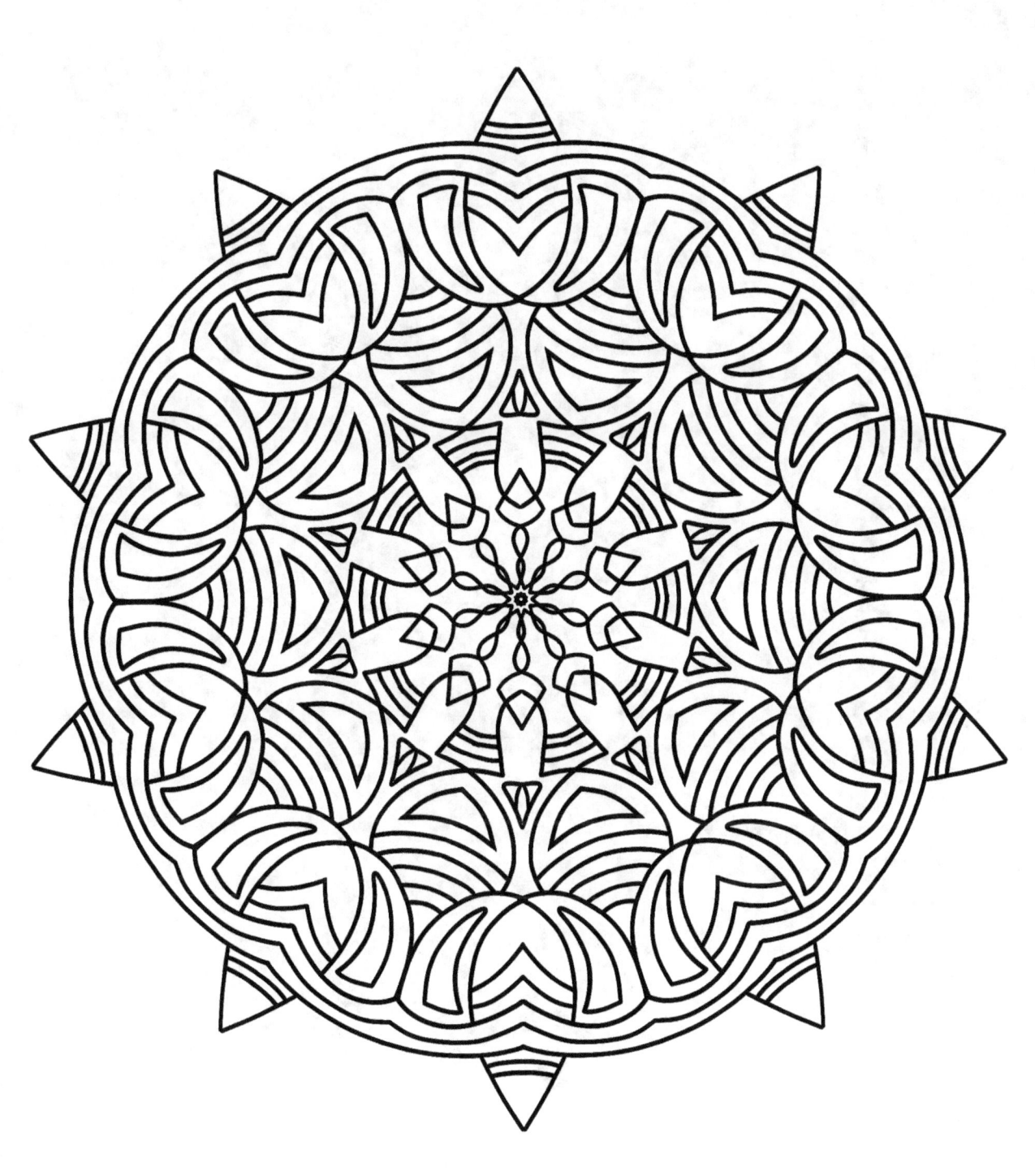

Hope you learned a thing or two.

Mandala level: Mandala master

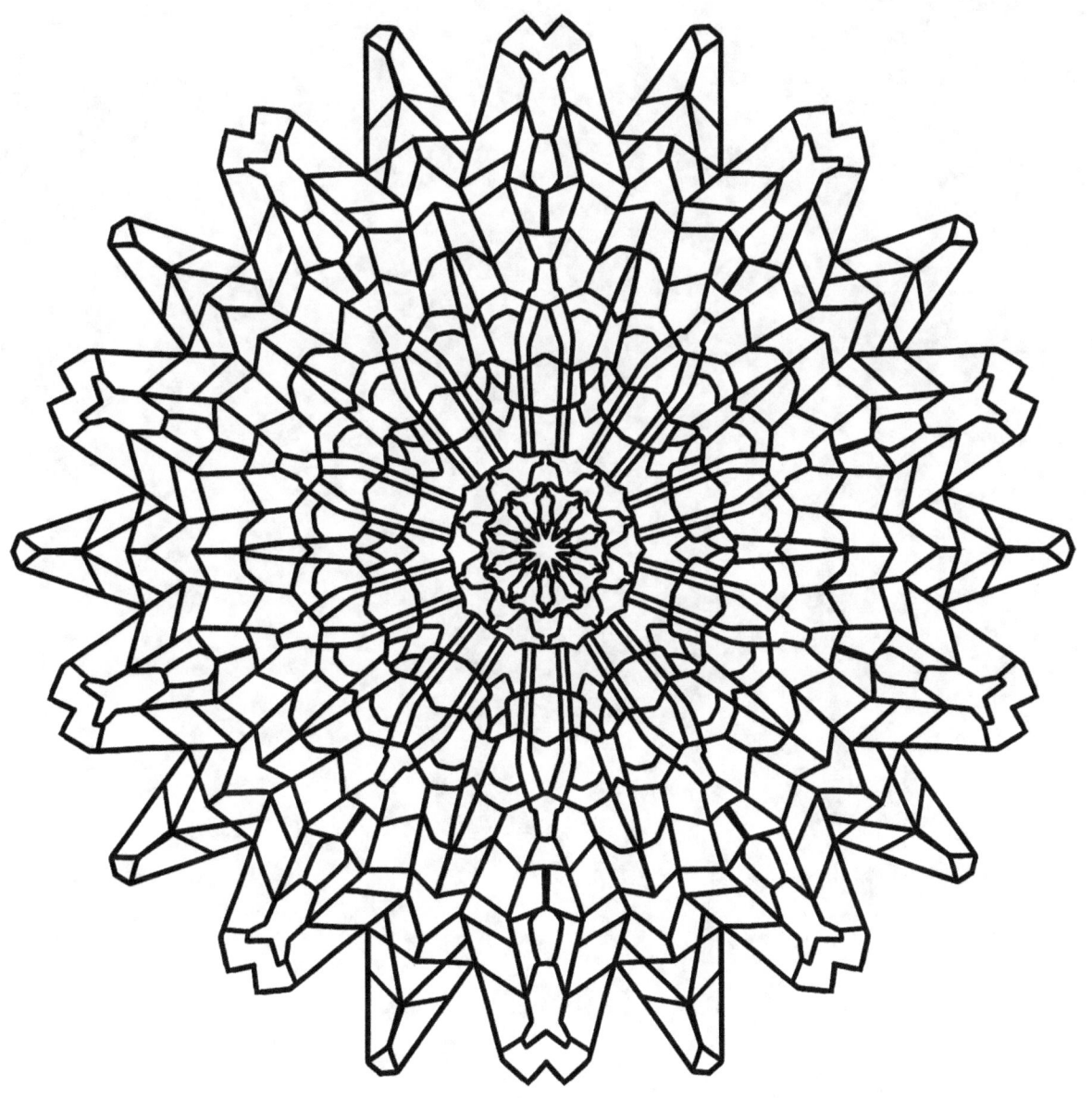

Well done. :)

Mandala level: Mandala master

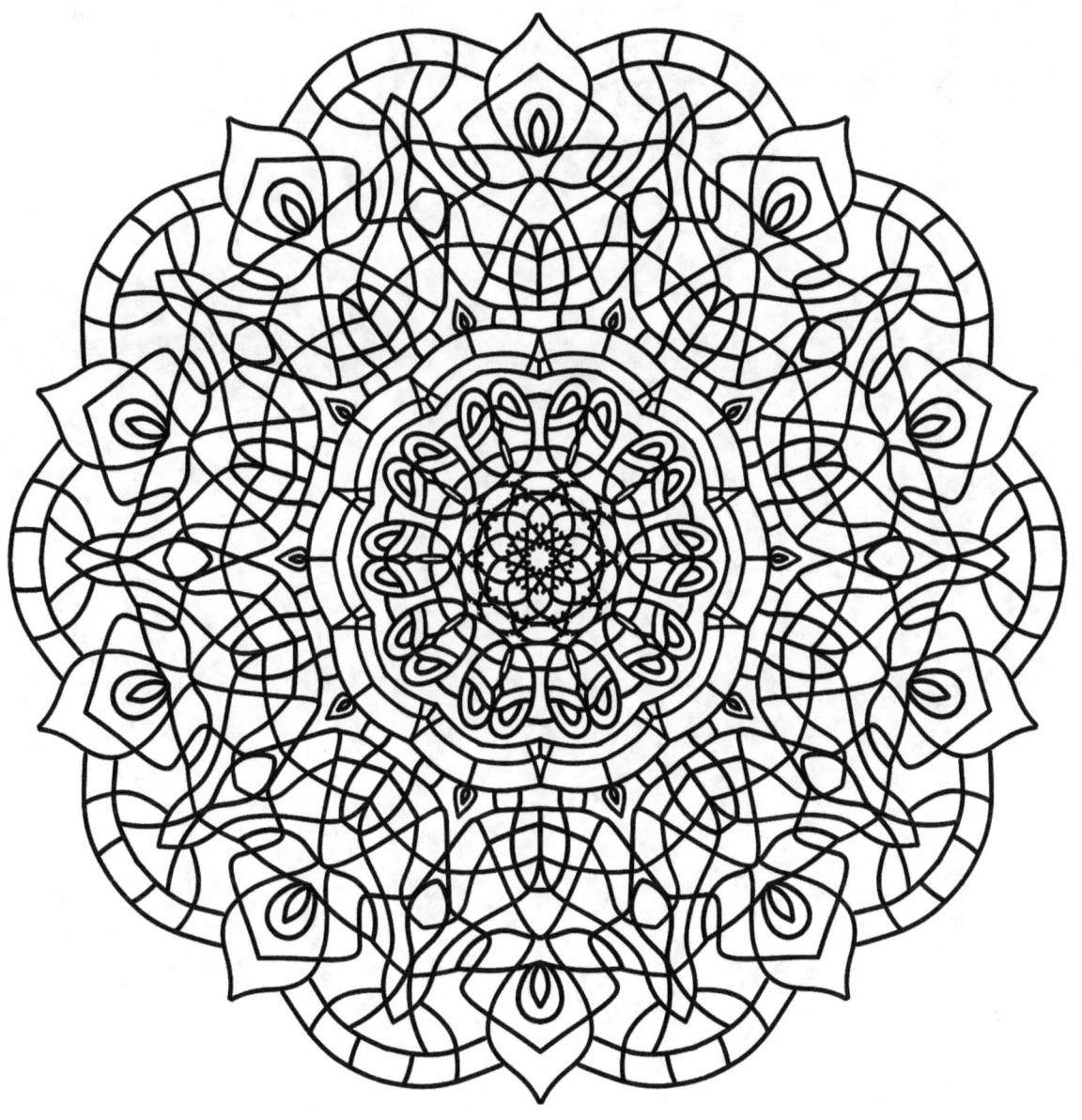

I'll miss you. It was a good run.

Mandala level: Mandala master

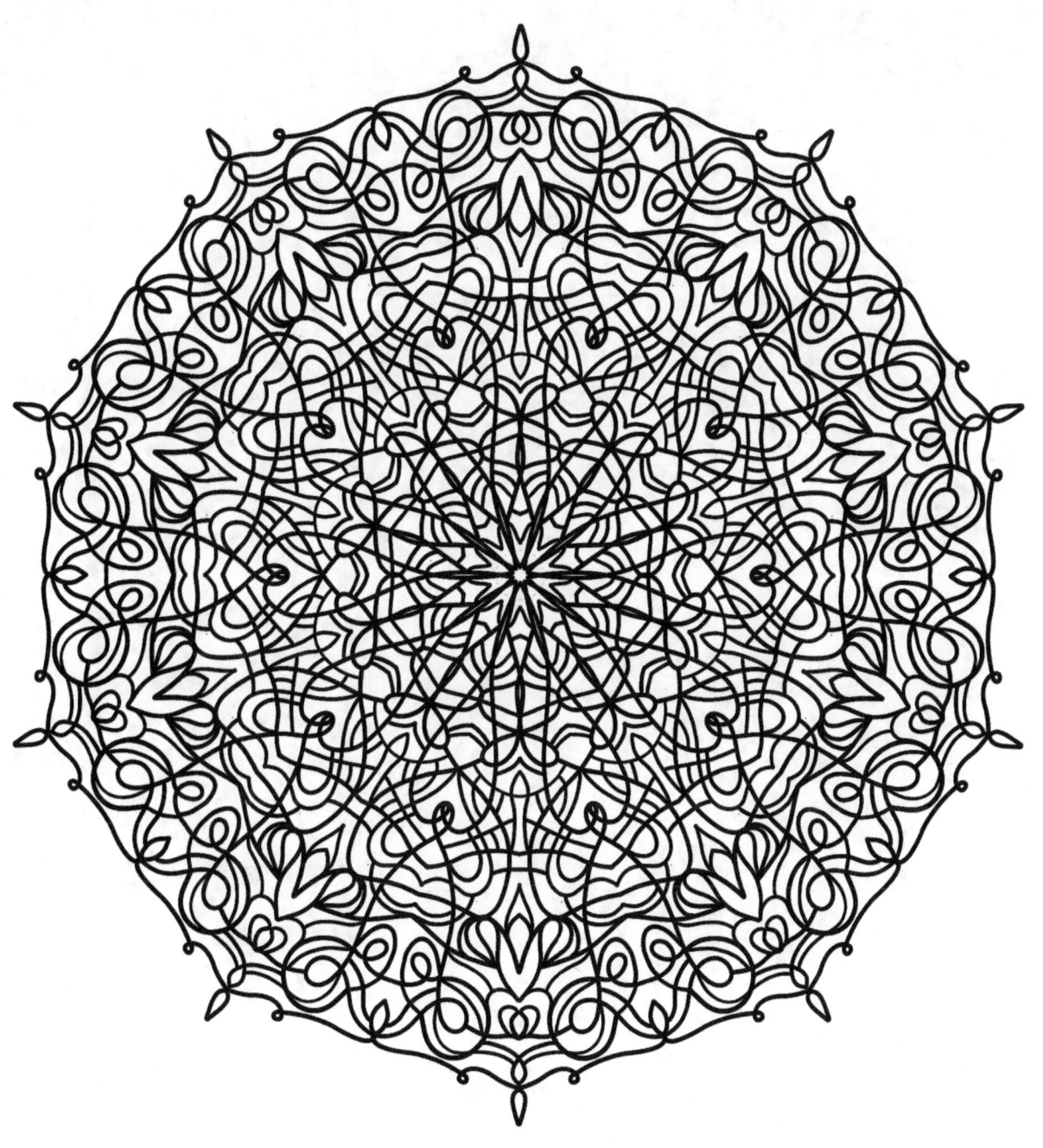

Eat your veggies. Stay hydrated. Don't throw stuff.

Mandala level: Mandala master

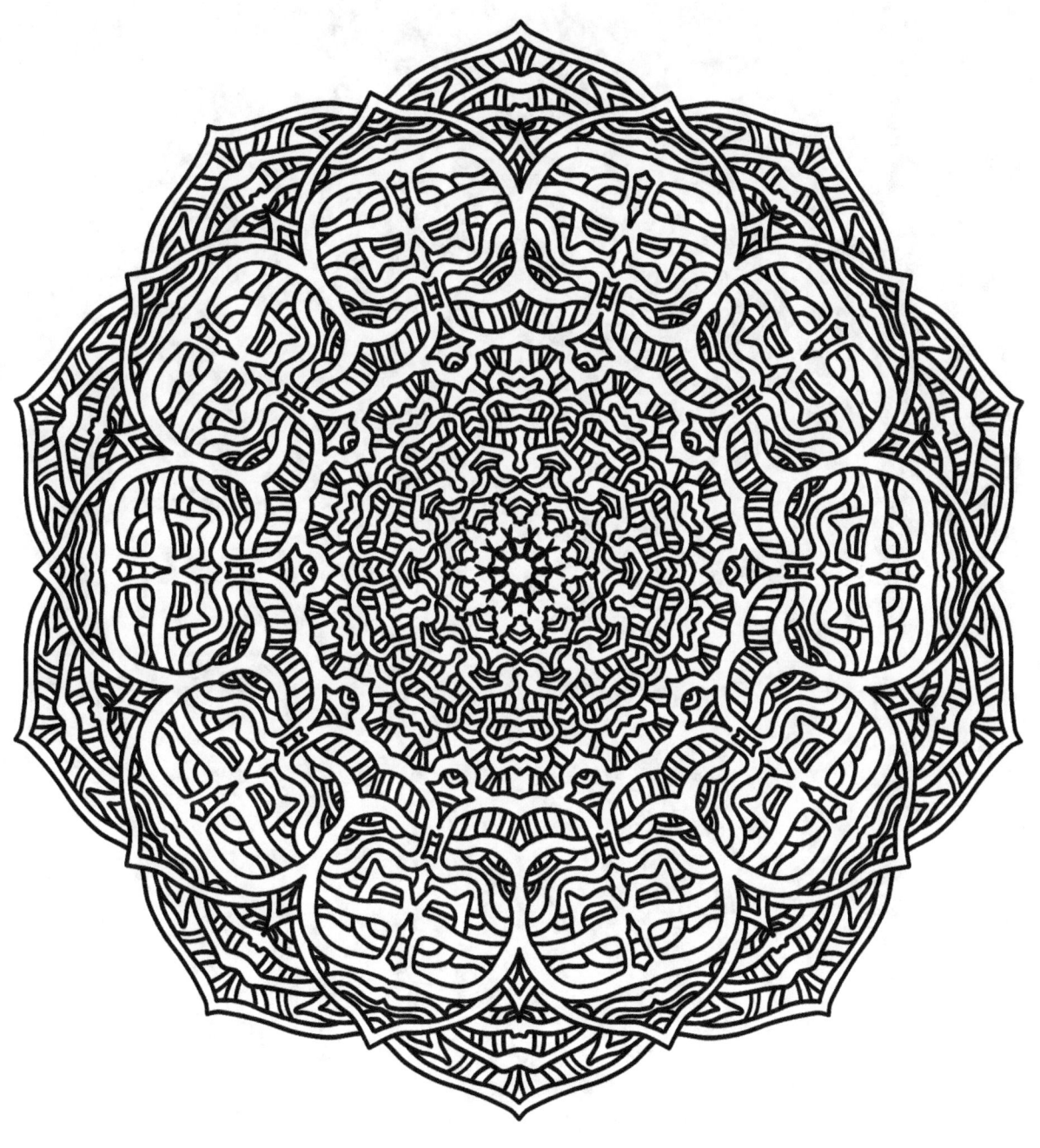

Thank you for listening. Stay safe.

Mandala level: Mandala master

Hello!

Glad to see you made it all the way here!
We've been waiting for you, so we could say: Thank you so very much!
By acquiring T(NS)RMB, you are encouraging our team to keep creating and designing more content for you.

We hope you had fun by letting us brighten your day a little bit (or let yourself brighten your day, since technically you did most of the job).
If this book made you smile, please, consider spreading the word by telling your friends, family or foes about it.

Also, now that you finished the book, you could add it to your resumé. It probably won't get you a job, but it might be a cool ice-breaker on those tedious interviews.

Hope to see you again soon!

    - The ArtsyGear team

P.S.
Actually, there are two kinds of whales:
- Odontocetes, which is only a fancy way of saying they have teeth.
- Baleen, who showed up late on the teeth distribution.
Instead of teeth, they have like a funky mustache where their prey gets stuck, in case you were wondering. You saw it here first.

Copyright © 2021-2022 by ArtsyGear. All rights reserved.

www.ingramcontent.com/pod-product-compliance
Lightning Source LLC
Chambersburg PA
CBHW060424220526
45465CB00008B/3004